'Cheap Date' Peter Blake

Cheap Date

Edited by Kira Jolliffe

ISBN 1 899866 26 4

Published in 2000 by
Slab-O-Concrete Publications
PO Box 148 • Hove • BN3 3DQ • UK
mail@slab-o-concrete.demon.co.uk
www.slab-o-concrete.demon.co.uk

Printed in Canada by
Hignell Book Printers Ltd

SQUASHED INTO THES

SQUARES YOU'LL FIND...

A Note From the Editor

Just in case you don't already know, *Cheap Date* is a phenomenon that has swept the Western World, converting the cognoscenti into wacky wallys. It's a magazine with a really, really small circulation, so here's a compilation of six issues that have been released so far, as well as a load of new stuff. It's a bit like a garage sale – you don't know *what* you'll find. Originally *Cheap Date* was basically about second hand clothes, but anti-fashion, anti-'lifestyle' and alternative consumer concepts followed soon after, and finally it became a big up-yours to something intangible but there. Hopefully we'll work that one out soon. Still, there's a whole lot goin' on inside!

xx **Kira**

Contributors

Peter Pavement is the publisher of this book. He's also the art director, proof reader and more. His contribution to this book mainly involved bending the reality of zillions of photographs – these include Exercise Machines (starring Nesta), Rachel Weisz's pin-up, Gaz's Socks, Jerry Hall's clouds and Putney Turner. He's the cut-out king.

Bay Garnett now edits New York *Cheap Date*. She's multi-faceted: a brillliant editor (she brought us The Coat and the Canadian ..., Harmony Korine's monologue, and Jerry Hall's pin-up among others), writer (check Big Foot), photographer (Chloe Sevigny), immaculately tasteful collector (see her T-shirts page) and, as you will see on page 55, she's MEAN.

Apart from being totally good looking and deserving cover-girl of *Cheap Date*, **Iris Palmer** is also a genius whose Dance Moves and Dead Good Looks only start to scratch the surface of her enormous ARSE – not really! – TALENT. She makes rare cameo appearances in Putney Turner and Beat Yer Friend at Charity Shopping. Oh yeah, and she and I made the cover T-shirt, but she did most of it while I laughed, and she delivered the Mary Poppins pin-up. Oh yeah! AND you'll need a doctor after you see HER pin-up.

Poppy de Villeneuve conceived and shot the Tale of Putney Turner, photographed Nesta's polkadot pin-up and the inside of Christopher Biggins' Home. She's in the middle of her first year studying photography, has an agent (Industry 0171 247 8778) and just remember you saw her stuff here first! See her Work Out on page 87.

Iain Aitch wrote most of the Obsolete? articles. Three steps ahead of everyone else culturally, he co-founded Decadent Action, is editor of *Fringecore* magazine and writer for just about everyone else, and is the most helpful person I know. I think.

Mini Weisz is studying graphic design. She did the evocative and

marvellous era-specific collages dotted around the book.

Anne-Marie Payne edits *Amp Minizine* which is small, pink, funny, interesting and for girls. It looks beautiful because of art director **Jake Ronay**, who also gave invaluable advice and ideas for the *Cheap Date* book. Anne-Marie interviewed Rosie about Food Skipping and wrote A Brief History of Knickers. Amp can be got by writing to PO Box 2286, London SE5 8WQ or check http://www.ampnet.co.uk. Get it!

Adrian Wilson shot Sophie Dahl and Poppy de Villeneuve's pin-up, the back cover and various other photos dotted around. The photograph of Sophie ended up in the National Portrait Gallery and deservingly won some award.

Rob Coyne is, strangely enough, a huge Marc Bolan fan. He, **Eugene** his brother and **Tim Lambert** produced The Story of Marc Bolan and with Hugo Martin make up **Mean Vincent** – a band which rocks the Universe.

Mark Pawson is generally thought to be God in an underground kind of way. As well as the important job of writing about his Swap Party

and Collection for *Cheap Date*, he's an artist, stall-holder, small-press distributor and racketeer. Disinfotainment, PO Box 664, London E3 4QR, UK. www.mpawson.demon.co.uk

Andrew Copeman's Budget Suave "punctuates" the book and reminds us of the discipline required to look really dapper – like he does.

It was really frustrating to not have room to publish all of **Patti Palladin**'s 22 handwritten pages of faxed answers to my questions so you can write to the publisher for the unedited version if you want to find out all about her childhood and what she's up to.

Nico van Harskamp writes about her ingenious club-based Super Swop Shop with photos by **Faye Norman** (0181 299 1798.)

Polly Devlin was born in Ireland, has written four novels and been awarded an OBE for Services to Literature. She writes about her fanatical collecting habit in The Bower Bird.

Francis Morgan is Binner. She's also an amazing dresser. To get the 'zine – contact us.

Scott Wishart, photographer,

reflects a typical car boot sale.

Stephen Drennan does the indispensable *Stephen's Little Book of Charity Shopping* and has started The 7 Inch Singles Club – call 01273 736 919. In his own inimitable style, he writes of his need for a tomato squeezy and about make-your-own records.

Alvin Smith is the great uncle of the 'zine scene. He was in the first ever issue of *Zig Zag*, danced on *Ready Steady Go* (you can see him in Donovan and Byrds footage), and writes here of his experience as an OXFAM sorter.

Polly Wiseman is actress, writer, independent theatre runner. She

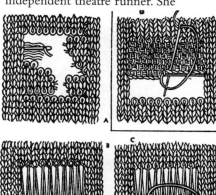

devised Shop Dropping.

Farah AlKalisi is one one the few people who've made a living out of sifting through charity shops to sell on to second hand clothes shops – pretty impressive! She's also a proper car nerd and I am sure we'll see her presenting *Go Faster!* or whetever, on TV soon.

Ayman Solene and **Chris Turner** are the clever men who've given us a historical perspective to the flea markets of Paris.

Bart Bealmear first wrote the Music and Marketing of Sigue Sigue Sputnik for US 'zine *Rebel Route*, PO Box 1740, Dearborn, MI48120-1740, USA.

Hugo Martin interviewed a professional blackjack player in The Stakis casino, which is where you'll find him when he's not playing poker

New Uses for Duffle Coat Buttons

at the Victoria Casino or playing guitar for Mean Vincent. Sometimes he comes home.

Lorna Miller, resident of Brighton, is a cartoonist and illustrator who has produced reams of highly distinctive comics, most notably her recent *Witch* book. Her artwork in Look Your Best At The Sea parodies those 30s annuals and in fact uses the genuine text from one edition.

Kelley Ryan lives in New York and knows all about good music. Here her quest to meet her heros is documented.

Charlotte Cooper is so clever and writes so clearly and is always interesting no matter what she writes about. Her A3 foldout 'zines are legendary and Found was one of them. She also wrote the Obsolete? article on Super 8. Write to her at 33 Romford Road, Stratford, London E15 4LY, UK Charlotte@ylwde.demon.co.uk

Jon Fortgang wrote I Was a Teenage Goth (which **Laura Findley** illustrated) and Museums of the Mundane and he should write a lot more.

Greg Rowlands gives us a guide to a few *Cheap Date* Yiddish terms while **George Parfitt** illustrates.

Cartoonist **Gray Jolliffe** invented 80s phenomenon *Wicked Willie*, did it to death, got bored of it and then had me force him to res'erect' its greatness for this book. Many years ago he also met my mum and with her produced

Maia, Jim and me. **Paul Pollock-Fitzgerald** and **Jane Lawson** run Enough – an anti-consumerist organisation and promoters of No Shop Day. Write c/o OWRIC, 6 Mount St, Manchester M2 5N3, UK for info.

Alex Freidman is the smart dude who wrote about The Bum Fund. Whatever career he choses, he'll be a great success.

Photographer **Huger Foote** has exhibited at Hamiltons. See his cute(!) photo of Yadira

Man of mystery **Gavin Clarke** is *Cheap Date*'s hunky mascot.

Tallboy really is tall. A great photographer, he shot Dressed to Kill and risked arrest in Shop Dropping – either for being illegal or for wearing a bright green plastic biker jacket.

Kym Canter is NY-based stylist-extraordinaire who produced the photos of Bay's T-shirts.

Legendary artist **Peter Blake** drew a *Cheap Date* logo for us.

One shouldn't need to explain who **Eric Goulden** aka Wreckless Eric is – buy any and all of his records. He played Graeme the dad (a bit *too* well maybe) in The Tale of Putney Turner, and gives us his refreshing Over-view. He has a band, Southern Domestic, is record producing and will also marry foreigners for money. Check out his wibsite at: www.bigsmash.co.uk.

Among photographer **Michael Woods**' work is the book *Paris and the Surreslists* with George Melly. He took pictures of George down the market in search of the surrealist spirit.

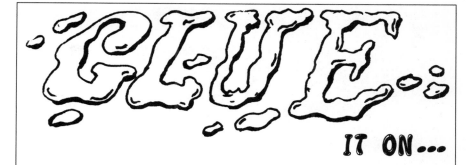

Copydex is a good glue for leather and feathers. Mix it with a load of glitter and apply to any fabric (apart from knits) with small paint brush. Superglue is good for jewellery. Bondaweb is a gauze with a thin layer of glue in it that melts and sticks when ironed. It's perfect for attaching fabric to fabric and prevents fraying. In fact, to save the bother hemming, iron some interface (one sided) along the edge. Plastic-look Fabric paints also make great glue. They come in most colours, glitter and pearly. Go nuts and squirt it all over your jeans, sticking anything to it as you go. **GLUE IT REAL GOOD!**

Sequence Your Sequins In Circles

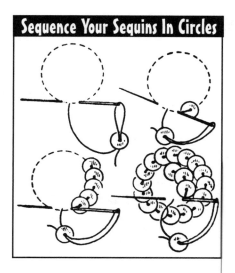

Thanks to our gorgeous pin-ups: **Nesta Fitzgerald, Emma Malin, Zoe Crowley, Kitty** and **Cicily Travers, Yadira Grant, Sophie Dahl, Jasmine Guinness, Rachel Weisz, Jerry Hall, Chloe Sevigny, Iris Palmer, Poppy de Villeneuve, Bay Garnett** and we wish Lucy, Mini and Anne-Marie were too!

Thanks to: **Matthew Wilkinson, Anita Pallenberg, Annabel Mullion, Anna Moulson, Dr Barnados Brixton, David Landau, Icky Hasmain, Gene Simmons, Chris Taylor, Christopher Biggins, Lucy Wood, George Melly, Marlon Richards, Tarka Cordell, Roger Burton, Lorna V, Mark Palmer, Ian Helliwell, Gaz Mayall, Nigel Mogg, Michel Houellebecq, Patrick King, Babsi, Lady Lucy, Aandy Garnett, Bella Shand, Marcella** at Scope, **Bernie, Max, Doune, Katie, Daisy de Villeneuve, John Lycett-Green.**

Thank you to **anyone else I've forgotten to mention**. Please fill in your name here: ....
....
....

BEAT YER FRIEND AT

1 By any means neccessary, make sure you're first inside the shop.

2 Case the joint in a few seconds. This ability comes with practice. Opening your Thrift Eye, either:
a) quickly spot the best looking 5 items and grab them without any pre-examination,
b) dive into the 50p basket/ bargain rail/personal speciality i.e. bags, toys, books, or...

2c) Remember what your friend's speciality is and get there before they do.

3 Remember this is a vicious competition. Pre-empt your friend's style. If you find a particular item that would only look good on them, buy it immediately. So what if it doesn't suit or fit you? Practice your innocent and hard-done-by looks when they glare at you. If they try this classic move on you, try to look non-plussed.

4 Take nothing they say at face value. You do not, and never will, suit a chunky boot or shoe.

5 Display the deep levels of your creative imagination by picking out a pair of gross items, running up to your shopping companion and shouting "Oh My God! This is SO you!! You must buy it! Go and try it on!" This is a great ploy, because they will never concede that you inhabit a higher level of irony (i.e. are better).

CHARITY SHOPPING

6 Confuse your shopping partner's taste. Insist that...
a) Airline paraphernalia
b) long nylon combat skirts
c) hip-hop gear
d) ugly cowboy boots
e) punk trousers and
f) 70s leatherette 'pimp' jackets are totally cool

7 By encouraging them to enter the fitting room, you are now free to rummage at leisure.

8 When you find the two of you sifting one rail, put your mental alarm bells at ease by shoving all the clothes along the rail so violently that they crush your mate's fingers in the process. Ow!

9 If all else fails, grab the Hall and Oates LP that your jumbling partner is smugly taking to the counter, right out of their hands, saying "I saw it first" then slink away. Be prepared to fight when they try to get it back.

10 Get home, realize the stuff you've bought is crap. Scheme up new ways to foist it all off on your mates (see 'I Had a Free Stuff Party' on page 32] providing they're still talking to you after the carnage you have wrought in today's Thrift War. But it doesn't really matter because you are the VICTOR!

**Kira Jolliffe &
Anne-Marie Payne**

GAZ'S SOCKS

" I go into shops and ask for rock'n'roll socks. Cheesy socks in both senses of the words. Stupid Cupid, Where have you Been All my Life? I'm Sex Mad, National Trust oak leaf socks I bought in Avebury. I was conceived in an oak tree.

Socks, they keep your toes warm.

For some people, the writing is on the wall. Me, it's written about the body. Everything sends some kind of message from the tip of my toes to the top of my hat. People think they're subtle, but they're sending out messages, I'm just

louder about it. I have no shame. I don't care what people think. Clothes are a canvas on which to create – I was never one for tattoos. Clothes are your outer skin, you can play around with that. I'm a colourful character from an artistic family. I'm creative and socks are an available canvas.

I had a weird phase as a kid at school. I was bullied because I was sent to school in short white socks and all I wanted was long grey socks like everyone else. I went to a jumble sale and got 'em and after a while I just thought they were fucking boring. The day I ditched 'em was the day I became a Teddy Boy. I didn't know if I was a mod or a rocker. One day I realized I was a modern rocker. I saw Teddy Boys wearing flourescent socks. They were loud and proud. I thought "Yeah, man, that's the way." and soon I had every colour of neon socks. Everyone always had short trousers so you were conscious of socks.

Come my birthday (29th December) or Christmas I've always got room for more rockin' socks (big ones, size 11). My brother wears tights, he's a cyclist.**"**

Any donations can be sent to: 615A Harrow Road, London W10.

EXERCISE MACHINES

Long before membership of your local gym was something you purchased on January the second and had lost under a pile of pizza cartons by February there was the home exercise plan.

These came in a variety of forms. Many were a twist on the Charles Atlas body building school. Exercise regimes that guaranteed that you would no longer have sand kicked in your face. These were rapidly followed by all kinds of gadgets from the chest expander – which looked like a kind of Slinky-based nipple remover – to the mighty Bullworker.

Of course 'the ladies' were not expected to build themselves up and take on strenuous exercise. But skinny was in and corsets were out so someone somewhere had the fantastic idea of shaking women fitter and thinner. It was often thought that young women needed a good shake anyway to rid them of the vapours. So this was ideal.

The machine in question consisted of a large belt which went around the waist. This was joined by a pole to a base which the subject stood upon. When plugged into the mains the belt could be adjusted to vibrate and shake your excess fat away at various speeds. Though on

reflection, they looked more likely to give you nasty stretch marks and bruises.

This machine became a regular feature of British comedy throughout the 60s and 70s, and it's a safe bet that Barbara Windsor was pictured shaking on one on at least one occasion. No doubt her top flew off as the machine shook out of control.

Obsolete? Well, like most home exercise gadgets this one was obsolete once it had left the box. How many times have your visited a friend who has a spare room or airing cupboard crammed with ThighMasters, Abdominisers, exercise bikes and the dreaded StepTM?

These lady-shakers don't tend to make it even as far as the junk shop or the book sale, and I recently saw two different models simply dumped on the street. Being the enterprising sort I have now set them up in my living room and I am pleased to offer discounted use of the facilities at my low-tech gym to ample-hipped readers of *Cheap Date*. Complimentary crisps, clothing optional.

Iain Aitch

Harmony Korine

Imagine the past lives of your second hand clothes. Harmony Korine does just that with some of Bay Garnett's recent finds.

White studded stained jacket

"This belonged to some big fuck Zoro guy with spandex. He is a spic and he plays three card monty, and I met him the summer of '78, and he tried to shuffle his dick a little too close to my stack and I didn't like him. He had a coif haircut and a fuckin' bad moustache job – he reminded me of a delinquent I knew from Arizona, named Hector Bebanko, who made films about runaways."

Red scrunchy jacket

"This jacket used to be owned by this girl named Charlese Sulemokee. She was a blood gangster. She was part of the blood faction in Compton. She had a 4 inch clit, that she used to fuckin' tittle. She got her neck shot out with a hypodermic that was marked fragile."

Top covered with glasses

"This used to belong to a nurse named Ned. He was a male nurse. He wore orthopaedic shoes and he was a fudge packer. He used to wear a cod piece. He was really into Hanna-Barbera cartoons, and he used to clip his hairs into a buzz cut, because he was jealous of people that were in the army, cause he was flat footed. His brother was a scientist who had a bad problem he's still trying to figure out."

Stilettos T-shirt

"This belonged to a little red riding hood apprentice from off Broadway, that used to listen to Jack Lemmon stand-up comedy, and she'd finger band herself with metal prongs. She used to go out with Dennis Hopper in, I guess it was his mish mash faze, right after he directed *Out Of the Blue*, but she was really spaced out because she was addicted to Zoloft and prescription pills. She had a... fuckin' dog she named Montreal after her favourite city in Quebec"

Interview and Photographs: Bay Garnett

FOOD SKIPPING

WITH ROSIE

"When I was squatting, it was just a part of the scene. People who were living there told me about the good runs, and took me there. Then I started going on my own. They were all supermarket skips: you had to climb over railings and squeeze through barbed wire to get to them. Quite dangerous. There's often little holes that have been prised open. The more difficult it is to get in, the more food you'll find. One time we found crates and crates of cider. It was leaking. Some were half full, some were empty but loads were intact. We didn't even take any, but it was piled high. They must have make the cans really badly or something. We've found cream cakes, bread... really gorgeous bread with jut and raisin in. Indian food. Parsnips and carrots. Loads of stuff, anything they sell in a supermarket, really. Haagen-Daz, Ben and Jerrys. It wasn't melted, we found it really soon after they threw it out. There's always lots of meat in there too, but no-one ever takes it. Cheese. Anything wrapped in polythene is fine, because you can just take it home and wash it off. Sometimes the stuff's going mouldy, but mostly it's just on the sell-by date, so it's fine.

I've never been ill from eating anything from a skip, only the first time we did it I had a bad stomach from eating too much! We got two carloads of food! We were eating as we were going through the skip, because it was the first time we'd ever done it and we thought it was a one-off.

Most of the skips now have changed into garbage gorgers. They have lids which are bolted down, so you have to get someone to break the padlock. Sometimes they forget to lock it. You have to climb inside garbage gorgers – it's really dark and dirty. When we first started doing it we had to wear old clothes and old shoes, because you'd get so much, and your hands smell. One skip in Leytonstone was full of sealed boxes. We were jumping up and down on the boxes and every so often a load of carrots or something would fly out, really fresh. That was the best skip ever.

It is illegal. I know people who've been chased by security guards. One time the guy who stacks the shelves came out. He was really young and didn't really get that was going on – he didn't know how to deal with it. He didn't really understand why anyone would be getting food from the skip. Another time a security man came out but we told him we were getting our dinner. He walked off and left us to it."

Best thing ever found in the street: "All my hi-fi equipment. TV, CD Player, amplifier, tape deck. everything works, though button on TV doesn't work properly. You have to press it really hard. Found it in the street, on the road."

Interview by Anne-Marie Payne

Confessions of an OXFAM Sorter...

Still impinged upon the nightmare of recent memory is the year which I served, courtesy of a government scheme, as an OXFAM pre-shop sorter, within a vast, dank warehouse (pigeons brazenly roosting in the rafters; triffid-like plants sprouting from the damp walls), incongruously set in one of Leed's leafier suburbs. Alongside idiosyncratic social outcasts and the brain-dead, my duties consisted of tearing open heavy p.v.c. bags out onto alarmingly mobile trestle-tables and sifting through the donated contents. Set against a continuous background of Radio Aire and dollops of enforced bonhomie, one's sole pleasure fixed upon the anticipatory chance discovery – that surrealistic juxtaposition which each package could reveal.

So then… a Ninja Turtle Pillow-case hiding blood-congealed syringes (my debut entry in the accident book and an enlightening afternoon in the out-patients department); four mildewed doorstep Dairylea sandwiches (one half-consumed); a pair of soiled knickers entangled around a plastic funeral wreath; an original clockwork Little Jimmy Osmond dancing-doll, complete with see-through packaging

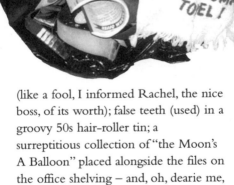

(like a fool, I informed Rachel, the nice boss, of its worth); false teeth (used) in a groovy 50s hair-roller tin; a surreptitious collection of "the Moon's A Balloon" placed alongside the files on the office shelving – and, oh, dearie me, dozens and dozens other treasures.

The gold medal, however, must be awarded to the discovery of a cat, lovingly wrapped within the folds of a pink, fluffy dressing-gown – and very much in an advanced condition of rigor mortis, though serene of expression and giving-off an aroma not unakin to ground ginger, seemingly captured in final, mid-flight leap. Attached to its tail by a knotted elastic band was a scrap of

paper reading: "PLEAS GIVE MERRY A DESUNT BERIAL THANK YOU". The feline was laid out upon the office settee and, whilst I scoffed down those Dairylea sarnies, we contemplated just what should happen next.

Despite the voluntary (sic) status granted to this scheme by the DHSS, I gained much satisfaction from my 12-month sojourn with OXFAM. Each of the more responsive discovered an individual niche leading to an enjoyable working day (I was given an hour or two on the books) and these compartmentalisations formed an unconscious whole of teamwork, as well as a friendly atmosphere: not to forget, of course, the opportunity to make a bid for goodies before they reached the shop.

From these worthy delegations came a marriage, a 70s-world emporium (run by the same couple), the best second hand record shop in Yorkshire, three shop managers and 2 of the dearest friends one could ever wish to know. It was a sad day when my year was up and I had no choice but to leave. Oh, and that Mr and Mrs now have a baby. Her name?? – why CHARITY, of course!!!

Alvin Smith

Continued on page 64

8-Track

The 8-track cartridge is the ugly kid brother of the compact cassette. Oversized and clumsy-looking, it was never destined to be loved by everyone, and sure enough, mass production ceased in the early eighties. The cartridges are dull-looking chunky slabs of plastic that hide the innovative figure-of-eight tape mechanism. Futuristic in that 70s way, they were the first format to experiment with skipping tracks, as you can now with Compact Discs.

The 8-track enjoyed far higher popularity in the US than in Britain, and that may be the reason for its revival (in an underground hipster way) over there. Vintage stores stock the brightly-coloured plastic models and the highly sought-after Panasonic 'Detonator' model. The tapes themselves are being snapped up in thrift stores for a few cents and appearing in collector's shops alongside Peewee Herman dolls and 'Brady Bunch' Memorabilia.

One man who may be kicking himself for all this is Russ Foster, who edits the zine *8-Track Mind* and created the low-budget movie *So Wrong They're Right*.

The film roadtrips across the US interviewing 8-track devotees and giving us the story behind the format. I was lucky enough to catch the film last year, and must say that I left hankering after my own player.

The players and cartridges can be found here at car boot sales and occasionally at charity shops. Some retro collectible shops have picked up on the fact that 8-track has a certain chic in its plastic awkwardness and sell them for £50 and more. But you really shouldn't pay over £20 for basic model and should be able to pick them up for a fiver if you trawl the boot sales. Cartridges shouldn't set you back much more than a quid, unless it happens to be a sought-after act like the Sex Pistols, The Beatles or Madonna.

Iain Aitch

8-Track Mind is available for $3 from 8-TM Publications, PO Box 90, East Detroit, MI 48021-0090, USA.
It is also carried in the UK by *Disinfotainment* – send an SAE to them at PO Box 664, London E3 4QR for their latest list of stuff.

Photograph: Chris Taylor

David Landau

Loot is ideal for CD readers. An alternative form of marketplace that doesn't make any judgements. How did Loot come about?

The idea started with me passing through the airport in Milan, I'd gone to see my mother in Lake Como. I picked up a paper called *2nd Hand*, thinking it was an antiques magazine – I'm interested in art, and in fact it was a free ad paper. I hadn't seen one before and read it on the plane and got very excited. I thought "Fantastic, this is going to be one thing that Londoners need, obviously there must be one in London, I've never seen one, I'll go and look for one." I looked in all newsagents on the way home in the taxi and none of them had ever heard of a free ad paper, so by the time I got home I was convinced I should start one.

As with all great ideas it's so simple.

As simple as could be.

Were you involved in publishing before that?

I was involved on a very small scale in the sense that I was the publisher of a scholarly art journal, quarterly, which I still do from home. It's a registered

charity and the leading journal in the world about the history of printmaking from the 15th century to the present, and it's heavy-going stuff. That was my only experience and *Loot* is obviously a completely different beast, but it gave me a slight feel.

Was it a fast learning process?

We learnt as we went along. Thankfully we didn't come from a publishing background, we started from scratch and put ourselves in the mind of the user, thinking we'd want something with lots in it; everything easy to be find, non-confusing design. The classifications were carefully thought out on the basis of what people need not by what tradition was, with 500 classifications instead of 4 or 5. We looked at all the competition like *Exchange and Mart* or

Daltons Weekly and they were so messy, you were lost in such a great heap of display advertising and couldn't actually find the ads and so in Loot the ads are free, which is the most fantastic thing. It's very very easy to advertise and our people, hopefully, are very nice, very efficient, very quick, it's not complicated and you get results. We built everything from the consumer's perspective, rather than saying "This is what we can offer and see if there's a market for it."

There's something quite hippie about the way *Loot* works.

It's a public service, it is, you know, so many people thought that we were a public service that we got a nomination for a special certificate as a public service which only applies to state owned companies. We had a letter from the Department of Employment. The fact that it was a public service played an enormous part in our decision to do it the way we've done it. The idea for me personally to get into business was to challenge myself, to prove to myself that in fact you could make money by never cheating anybody. Before I got into business I thought that this was not possible, that businessmen were all crooks and they were just taking

founder of **Loot**

innocent people who were paying £20 for something when they could have paid £10 for it, which is often the case. That's why you have a magazine about it. I was speaking about this with my mother at some point and she said "You can make money by being honest." So I thought, if I ever get an idea that I think really is fantastic; a cracking idea that would really send me wild, that I'd do it, apply this methodology and never swindle. I'd never charge more than is fair, I'd just want to make money out of it, I want it to be a profit-making enterprise. I can look into the eyes of my customers and say "Yes I've done this I've done that, the reason why I'm charging you this is because of that" and it's open and fair.

Have your opinions changed then?

I think that people don't realise how hard it is to do business, it's not that 'by dint of being in business, you're going to make money' – that's not true. Many people work very hard that produce some beautiful things, beautiful services, and they make no or very little money. Many people have a hard time going through business. It's also fair to say there are plenty of crooks around. Plenty of people who have no

principles, or they have them but don't apply them, but I think they will die out in due course because people thankfully are more and more aware of what their rights are, and are less and less willing to be taken to the cleaners, and because communication is getting so much easier, and interaction with products is getting so much more lively of late. I've not changed my mind about the importance of being honest, now I know it works which is reassuring. It is difficult because the more bigger the group of people in a company the more difficult it is to maintain these lines.

What's your history?

I was a medical doctor and studied cardiology, and then I left that because I thought that what I was doing was the wrong approach to medicine and at that time holistic medicine was not that fashionable. I then wrote a book about a German printmaker and a friend suggested I apply for a fellowship in printmaking at Oxford. I did as a joke because I had not qualifications and got it! I still teach there.

Are you quite political?

I was a convinced Marxist-Leninist when I was 17. I was on the barricades

being beaten by the police every day. Fundamentally I am socialist, though even now labels don't mean very much these days, and I don't attach this label to my way of thinking, I just like fairness. I don't like injustice, prejudice, discrimination so if I have to fight against them I do.

Loot is particularily good because it has created an entirely new and democtratic marketplace. Does that feel like a responisiblity?

We have really created a new market that didn't exist before because nobody would advertise a 2nd hand fridge or chair before because it would cost £30 to advertise a chair that you would sell at £20. It is a great responsibility. The important thing is to think of ourselves as technically the intermediaries for the general public. We give them a way, a medium to do what they want to do, rather than tell them what to do, what's good for them. Ultimately in the process we make money. It's really, really useful.

It's also a unique noticeboard.

A slice of London with 25,000 advertisers every day. Some are really weird, some completely normal.

Whilst in Blatchington Road, Hove, almost fourteen months back, I popped into the Red Cross shop, emerging triumphant - or at least with curiosity aroused - with a 50p one-sided 7 inch, housed for protection inside an old green-&-white Parlophone sleeve ... pretty bashed and battered, and with no indication as to its content - but with its white printed-on label bearing the legend "Calibre auto recording", I guessed - correctly, as it turned out - that I'd stumbled upon an example of the long-forgotten art of amateur record-making (if you're familiar with Brighton Rock you'll perhaps recall that special recording facilities once existed in seaside resorts). Back home, I excitedly shoved said 45 onto my turntable, and was greeted with a host of pops and clicks, and then a male voice ... distorted and crackly where the singing was too lusty and loud. Wow - this guy really swung, Sinatra-style. Commencing, "I've just found joy / I'm as happy as a baby boy", and with lines including, "This heart of mine / Was doing very well / The world was fine / As far as I could tell / And then suddenly I met you ...", this was classic '40s/'50s Radio 2 stuff of the type endorsed by the rock and roll-opposing Vic Godard. An unaccompanied rendition (not certain just how spacious or otherwise those booths were - could, say, a guitar have been accommodated ?) with other folk audible in the background - passers-by, kids shrieking, perhaps friends/family conversing expectantly outside...

These discs seem to have been of a limited length - sadly, the song here was chopped off in full flow, never reaching its crescendo/conclusion. I've seldom seen - let alone purchased - auto recordings : perhaps people embarrassedly kept them at the back of a drawer, too sentimental to coldheartedly chuck away their souvenirs of devil-may-care, spontaneous holiday fun. Maybe not so many existed - were they too expensive to get made, except as a luxury/indulgence on a special occasion? But this particular example is just great - no personality cult, no media hype, no ad campaigns fostering feelings of insecurity and fear of odd-one-out ridicule ... nothing more or less than pure 'n' simple seaside (?) expression shining through the skips, the several blocks past which the needle refuses to sail, and the surface fizz. Time for a compilation of such gems ??

Iris Palmer's DANCE

The Totally Off-Centred, Paranoid Individual's Experience of the Dance Floor

Freak out inwardly.
Cringe and writhe.
If you get into the cringing and writhing, it's fun. (For sure, believe me!)
Music: 'Rapper's Delight'

Mosh/Pogo

Music: The very good, also a very good reaction to the very bad.

The Pervert Dance

Hovering around the butt-area, or even clinging pelvically onto the side of an unaware female.
Can be done in groups of three.
Female preferably 16 years old and off her face on Ecstasy.
Music: 'I Like it Raw'
Busta Rhymes.

Black Lace – Superman

The easiest dance to achieve.
Just follow those crazy instructions, and eat shit.
It's fun! and good exercise too!
Music: 'Superman'
Black Lace

MOVES

photos: Poppy de Villeneuve

actors: Matthew Wilkinson

Patrick King – poet,

Kira Jolliffe,

Poppy de Villeneuve

Iris Palmer

The Jig Yer Tits In A Vest Top, With Great Hair, and Loads of Foundation (Or Loads of Hair and Grreatt Foundation!!)

(uh, yuh?! – ed)
Keep chatting to your girlfriends with a concerned look on your face.
Hands raised with pack of cigarettes in one.
Music: 'Virtual Insanity' Jamiroquai

Wank on Space or Space Wanker

Miming your way out of a giant soap bubble, go up as close as possible to the light show. Let those crazy patterns play on your closed eyelids, as they reveal cosmic realities.
To you.
Music: Any music.

The Old Guy in the Street Doing an Impromptu Tap-Dance

Music: a memory of the good ol' days

The Punk Destruction Waltz

Take your partner, throw her violently onto (into) the boogy-ing bunch about you.
May she land, graciously,... like a ton of bricks, only to jump up, and head-butt you.
Proceed in a waltz-like action, alternately.
Music: 'I Can't Live, if Living is Without You' Nilssen

The PVC, Sweat & Ecstasy

Takes three people who are willing
to get physical.
Doesn't matter what sex.
Have a rhythmic and funky sexual
innuendo get-down.
Pour with sweat and roll your eyes
to animal heaven.
And grind your teeth down.
Music: 'Erotica'
Madonna

Modern Dance

is a totally emotional, raw dance.
Follow that beautifully erratic path of
your emotions – Feel it, and express it.
Pay no attention to the music playing at
all, or compose your own in your most
private moments, and bring it along.
Encourage people to join in and
represent your deepest fears and
fantasies, expressed in the form of a
dance montage.

The Shy (or Slightly Older Straight) Guy

who kicks up a crazie fuss on the
dance floor, at 80s nightclub, on
first date with secretary. In movie.
Music: "She's a Maniac"
Hall and Oates?
"Let's Hear it for the Boy"
Footloose soundtrack.

Attempted and Failed Break Dance

Is always funnier than serious –
although serious is fantastic! Get over-
excited and jump into the splits to start
your routine. Get stuck there and rip
your suit trousers cos you are too fat.
10/10 for enthusiasm (do it again yeah!!)
Music: 'Rapper's Delight'

The Side-Stepping of Mothers

at the primary school disco, when
they come to pick everybody up at
the end.
Music: 'Relax'
Frankie Goes To Hollywood
'I Can Feel It In
the Air Tonight'
Genesis

A *Cheap Date* promotion

Safety Pins

They're beautiful things.

The safety pin was invented in 1849 by Saint Walter Hunt of America after fiddling with a piece of wire for a couple of hours. He sold the patent for $400.

The miracle of the safety pin.

Just some of the things you can acheive:

1 With 3, a large enough piece of material and much improvisation, make: skirt/top/dress/hat. For extra sophistication, use scissors. Ladies, for modesty, cut your tight's legs off at the knees and a hole in gusset to wear as top. Cut holes in toes of leftover for belt/hat/ankle warmers. What, an outfit.

2 Fill the prongs of enough (about 50) safety pins with beads and string 2 strong pieces of elastic through them to make a *wonderful* bracelet/anklet.

3 Pin the sleeves of your T-shirt to the shoulder – cute little bunched up sleeves!

4 Arbitrarily bunch up material in plain, ill-fitting garment. Suddenly it looks expensive.

5 Stick one through your lip. Go on!

6 Pin through back of material (typically, your sweatshirt) and thread a feather through the front.

7 Keep yer high-tops on with big ones through lace holes.

8 Make a really really long chain out of them for belt, choker, fun.

9 Make falling-apart clothes wearable for another day.

I had a FREE STUFF PARTY

Everyone's got piles of stuff they don't need or want anymore. Think of all those records & CD's you haven't listened to in years, the books you're never, ever going to re-read, all those clothes that don't fit and are unlikely to ever come back into fashion and home furnishings that now look like remnants of past lives. I'm sure *Cheap Date* readers are aware of this phenomena – messy piles of stuff buried at the back of the wardrobe, cardboard boxes of junk in the cupboard under the stairs that you've been intending to do a car boot sale stall with for the last four years, and what about that tea chest up in the loft that you haven't unpacked since you moved house?

Why do we hang onto these disposessed posessions and belongings that don't belong anymore? I think there's a certain strata of stuff which is just a bit too good to throw away – stuff we kind of want to dispose of but hold onto at the same time. If only there were good homes for it all to go to.

I think there should be neighbourhood swapshops, warehouses where you take unwanted stuff and exchange it (if you want) for other stuff on a number of items or equal weight/volume basis, either free or for a nominal charge. Following the reduce-reuse-recycle mantra, Reusing things-by finding new homes or uses for them, is more ethical and practical than much-publicized recycling schemes.

Well anyway, earlier this year I decided to do my bit to solve the global tide of unwanted and unloved stuff by holding a FREE STUFF PARTY. Everyone I know lives surrounded by stuff in cluttered living spaces which are the exact opposite of (John) Pawsonesque minimalism, so I was sure the 30 invited friends would all have stuff to get rid of.

The date was set for April 2nd, and invites posted three weeks beforehand, giving people plenty of time to do some spring cleaning and sort stuff out. The invitation was carefully worded to ensure that everyone actively took part and brought stuff – no freeloaders! Everyone I spoke to before the party said they'd been sorting stuff out, and were looking forward to the FREE STUFF PARTY.

As the day approached I felt a bit nervous. Would my house get stripped of its contents? Would I be engulfed in heaps of rubbish afterwards? I realised that the setting swap party idea in

FREE STUFF PARTY

You're invited to Mark P's Free Stuff Party on Friday April 2nd 1999

It's time to have a spring clear-out and bring your unwanted gifts, fashion mistakes, all those books and records that you know you'll never read or listen to again, that box full of junk that you've had in the cupboard since you moved house intending to do a carboot sale with... ABSOLUTELY ANYTHING that someone else might have a use for-if you don't want it we do!

Here's how it works: Arrive from 7pm onwards, bring stuff in bags or sealed boxes so that nobody gets a peek in advance. Everything will be piled up. The Free-for-all frenzy will start at 9pm everyone can pile into the moutain of free stuff, ripping bags open and grabbing whatever catches their eye - there'll be plenty of time afterwards to swop and trade, model your new outfit and see what everyone else got.

Black Bin Bags will be provided for you to get your booty home. Anything left over will be taken to a charity shop. Strict door policy. No Stuff, No Entry!

Remember Kids-it's much better to Reuse than Recycle...

and SURVIVED!!

motion was an experiment, I had very little control over what happened, and no real idea way of what it was going to be like!

On the evening people arrived bringing anything from a car full of boxes to a handful of objects in a carrier bag. We piled books and records in the front room, clothes in the bedroom, and everything else in the kitchen, each room soon had its own impressive mountain of bags & boxes with a few items tantalisingly poking out.

At 9.30 my noisiest wake-the-whole-house-and-the-neighbours alarm clock went off heralding the start of the free stuff frenzy, everyone scampered off into different rooms ripping boxes apart and tearing plastic bags open... people were soon roaming around with arms full of new acquisitions and rapidly filling up bin bags.

This snapping-stuff-up period went in two waves, there was an initial energetic grabbing frenzy followed by a more leisurely browsing phase, as people realised there was still undiscovered stuff in other rooms, it was nice that this lasted for a while, rather than being all over and done in five or ten minutes. It was great fun getting people to try their new clothes on, show you what they'd got and what you'd missed out on.

Everyone had a great time, and went home clutching piles of stuff delighted with their acquisitions, even the couple of guests who'd come intending just to get rid of things couldn't resist temptation! There seemed to be extra satisfaction gained from stuff being utterly FREE, more exciting than the cheapest bargain in the sales or the most unexpected junkshop bargain!

Late that night, I heaved a mountain of strange clothes off my bed and happily went to sleep, only to be woken early the next morning by the doorbell ringing, I staggered up but couldn't find any clothes to put on- where I'd left my jeans the night before were three pairs of girls 28" waist jeans!

It took 2 days to clear up, and about the same time to unpack all the stuff I'd stashed away to make room for the party! Debris and leftovers were strewn everywhere, and when collected together, filled 4 binbags of clothing & shoes plus a big box of books and junk. The clothes went into the local Dr Barnados clothes bank, books into the paper recycling collection, and everything else into the

Photograph: Adrian Wilson

dustbin. O.K. I'm sorry, I apologise, I know the invitations promised that all leftovers would go to a charity shop, but the leftovers were real rubbish that I'd have been embarassed to give to a chartity shop – they'd have just thrown it out anyway.

The Free Stuff Party was definitely a success. I'd encourage anyone thinking about having their own party to go ahead and do it – the only thing I'd change would be to have a more organised show and spend part of the evening getting everyone to show off what they'd got.

I'll definitely do it again, maybe in a couple of years time, not annually, that would just get predictable, although having said that I've already started putting stuff aside for a future Free Stuff party and know a few other people have as well. I think it would be interesting to see how a Free Stuff Party would work on a larger scale in a bigger space with everything in a single central pile.

Mark Pawson

Michel Houellebecq...

An nterview with the controversial French novelist.

I heard you have a hatred of consumerism

That's true but you read the book. What I dislike is advertising. For me I have worked several years in computer systems. It's a good subject for a book, because it's important. Another subject which is better is advertising, but I don't really know this world. I have a friend which has worked seven years I think in advertising and I always tell him to write a book, because it's a great subject.

Why do you hate advertising?

Because first, desire is a normal process but advertising increases desire too much. The second point is that advertising must always be new, and life is not always new. I think that now advertising vampirise desire. You will never be satisfied, because you must always desire something new. Advertising is a machine to make desire, to develop frustration but not to make satisfaction. Truth and desire have been killed by advertising. Now our desires are advertising desires. We are becoming something new. We are something false.

Do you think it makes us slaves?

Yes yes. The word is not too strong. Slaves, yes. You can say that. Yes.

Who is the enemy?

Enemies. No. It's a strange thing, because there is no enemy. People are just doing their job because they need money. They produce useless things, they produce desire for useless things. Nobody's bad.

In the book you say a lot of your time is taken up having to do things. Abiding rules. Is it symptomatic of the same thing?

Not really the same thing. The point is that there is much unemployment in France and in Britain. When you've got a job, it takes much energy. Suddenly, you discover that you're giving energy to things that doesn't interest you. Deeply. When you go in a supermarket, it's a complicated process, because you think you want to buy a good produce, good for your health and not much money and you want to eat something that you like. Sometimes you think of these things and you panic, because there is too much information. It's no pleasure.

Is that particular of now?

Yes it's getting worse and worse, slowly.

Can you see it coming to a head at some point in the future?

I am unable to make prophesies, but it's very strange because I like science and technology, it's good for progress, but it's strange to have more and more technology, to work more and more and to have less and less satisfaction. It's very curious, very difficult to explain.

Maybe to help to explain it, can you imagine a utopia.

No I'm not able to do that. Because the problem of production of goods can not be sold on utopia's shelf. As a pessimist I don't think the appetite for money is the only motivation, there is another strange reason. I think it will be much clearer in the film.

Have you written the screenplay?

Yes with the director, Philippe Garelle.

Jerry

...Dreamy

George

**Photographs by
Michael Woods**

Whenever I need to reinforce the surrealist spirit, I stroll down Portobello Market, and search the stalls for objects which transcend the mundane routine of life, like shopping, into a world of the Marvelous. And of course, there's the "chance encounter".

But first, a quick salute to my navy days, and although I never saw active service in the conventional sense, nor did this model battleship, but an interesting toy for the bath tub all the same!

You may think, with justification, that including the Telly Tubbies, and no jibes that I resemble one, is stretching Surrealism to its limits, but don't they inhabit an imaginary world bordering on the absurd. Possibly more Lala, or is it Dada? That surrealism, but what an antidote to "Blind Date"!

Melly

Imagine, even the most ordinary household objects, such as this plastic apple, presumably an ice-bucket, when put in front of the face, immediately conjures up Magritte. "Anyone got a bowler hat?"

Age not being a factor, the female form, in all its representations, never fails to arouse me, and true to form, I react instinctively whenever one becomes available. Sexuality, so they say, is all in the mind, and given the sorry state of this headless torso, it'll have to stay there! Now, what did my wife ask me to buy? Oh yes, six oranges, and as for my surreal escapades, "Don't tell Diane".

George Melly, *Don't Tell Sybil: An Intimate Memoir of E.L.T. Mesens*, is published by Heinemann, at £17.99

I ♥ Super 8

Super 8 is a type of 8mm cine-film that became popular during the 1950s, 60s and the early 70s when people made and bought home movies. Home entertaining seemed to have grandiose ideas above its station during this period; why ever go out when you could emulate a restaurant with your hostess trolley, serve cocktails from behind your home bar, and retire to your own private cinema as long as the projector didn't break down (again). This lifestyle could not be sustained and the latter luxury fell from grace when cheaper and more immediate video technology became accessible. Although it is still manufactured, Super 8 is now I think almost solely in the hands of nerdy collectors, film students, and retro freaks.

Super 8 has its own particular hardware. I have notice the occasional camera in charity shops but they have rarely worked. I think that should you want to indulge yourself in the world of home cinema then your best bet is to go to a specialist shop, they often have cheap second-hand equipment, or buy *LOOT*, or look in the small ads of you local paper, which is how me and Simon got hold of ours. We found a camera, projector, projecting table, screen, editor, and splicer for fifty quid from this guy who had retired and was moving house. Like many people he wanted to discard his old film-making gear because he reckoned it was obsolete and that video and modern technology was better. We went to his house to pick it all up, he demonstrated how to make the projector work by showing us some footage he had shot of his wife sunbathing topless in Torremolinos one summer a long time ago. Our jaws dropped as we watched her slumped on the beach whilst jumbo-jets landed behind enormous white hotels in the background. It was all so fabulously modern. When the film was over the man said he'd give us some spare spools, and we watched in horror as he dumped film after precious film on the floor, then handed us over the empty plastic inserts. It was as though he thought that his life and his memories were over. Later that day we made a solemn vow to treasure our films until the end of our days.

Okay, so once you have your hardware you need something to shoot on it. Sometimes you come across

Thanks to Ian Helliwell for Super 8 film stock

an old stash of unwanted films in second hand shops, but beware, charity shop pricing is random, some shop workers remember Super 8 as a desirable commodity, others think of it as useless and price it accordingly, though a new generation of volunteers sees fund-raising opportunity in its retro value. Simon and I used to live near Clear Vue in Stroud Green Road in North London. This was an old style camera shop run by a three misfits which smelled of fag smoke, there were big glass bowls of Pick 'n' Mix on the counter, and little hand-written price tags on a dazzling variety of equipment. The shop closed about five years ago because one of the proprietors died and the others could not continue without him, but me and Sime spent many happy times cruising the back room for forgotten films. We found *Batman* cartoons; 8-minute silent Super 8 versions of *Shaft* and lurid horror films; *Bucket of Blood*, *Straitjacket*, *Dr Cyclops*, *Squirm*; travelogues of Walt Disney World and a *Royal Tour of Tonga* (featuring full-on cheek piercing!); strange outdated anthropological films like *Life With the Pygmies*. Sometimes we found stag films, models such as the black-eyed Jayne Tracey in big bouffant wigs T-A-K-I-N-G O-F-F T-H-E-I-R U-N-D-E-R-W-E-A-R- and posing luxuriously. These smutting delights were always my favourites. Maybe there's a shop like this near you. Or maybe you should check out the biannual Cine Collector's Fair at Ealing Town Hall which is run and attended almost entirely by obsessive sweaty oddballs in anoraks. You'll feel right at home.

So far I've mentioned only commercially produced Super 8, but there's another type of film for which I am always on the look-out. These are the home-made films that people clear out of their attics and donate to charity shops. I can barely describe the poignancy of witnessing in flickering light the private memories of people you will never know; a first holiday taken together in the caravan, now babies being paraded outside the maternity wing, a man with huge sideburns welcoming the viewer to his new house, messing around at your last school Sports Day. My favourite found film of all time is half an hour of a young man and his proud parents and beautiful older sister welcoming an endless stream of crazy, wildly-dressed relatives to his bar mitzvah. The year: 1972? Wow! These grainy little films somehow become memories of your own foggy past life. Although Super 8 films can be expensive to make, and you still have to send away your cartridge for processing, they also have this quality of faded remembrance which is not found in the cleaner lines of video. It is this instant nostalgia which attracts me to Super 8 and I am reminded of the time it snowed one winter and we filmed each other rolling around in the changed landscape, breaking off icicles and throwing snowballs. Within a week the snow had cleared and the weather brightened. Within another week our film had returned from Kodak. When projected it took on the quality of iconic domestic history, it looked like it had been shot years before. We appeared younger, more radiant, healthier, happier, funnier than now. Who wouldn't want to see themselves like this? This is the power of Super 8.

Charlotte Cooper

Bay's T Shirts

These are just some of Bay Garnett's amazing collection of T-shirts from the thrift stores of New York. Send £10/$10 to: 434 Broadway, Suite 406, NY NY 10013, USA and she'll send you her next purchase. Particular styles obviously can't be catered for – you'll just have to rely on her immaculate taste!

Chloe...
New York Doll
...Deeelicious!!

Photograph: Bay Garnet

Cheap Date

Christopher Biggins

Style guru Christopher Biggins kindly invites *Cheap Date* into his house and wardrobe.

He only wears red socks "They look good with everything."

Kaftans: men could wear them more often. "They're so comfortable on holiday."

"I am still big its the pants that get small"

Biggins after breakfast in his kitchen.

Joan Collins and Christopher are best briends, going back a long way.

3D portrait using one of Biggins' actual shirts.

Diamante on jacket shoulder "looks like a very expensive bird dropping!"

Photographs: Poppy De Villeneuve

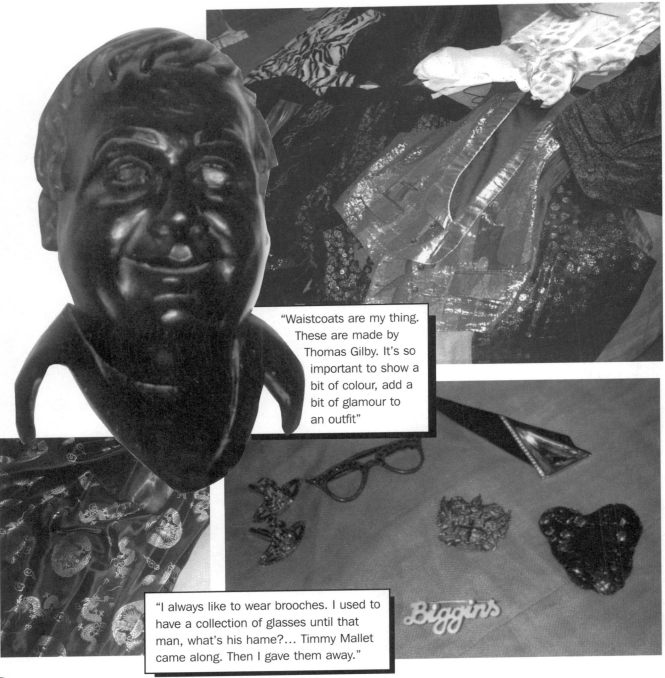

"Waistcoats are my thing. These are made by Thomas Gilby. It's so important to show a bit of colour, add a bit of glamour to an outfit"

"I always like to wear brooches. I used to have a collection of glasses until that man, what's his hame?... Timmy Mallet came along. Then I gave them away."

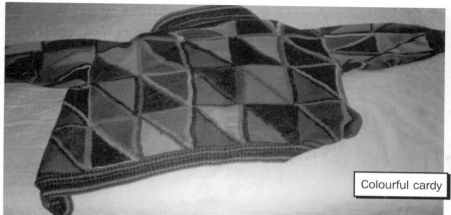

Colourful cardy

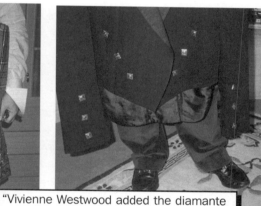

"Vivienne Westwood added the diamante at the bottom for me"

Sumptuous black velvet jacket with yellow satin lining

Buy It Flaunt It

the music and marketing of

Named after a Soviet pick-pocket gang, Sigue Sigue Sputnik descended on the British music industry with an unprecedented marketing campaign designed to create the ultimate rock'n'roll supergroup. It failed. "This is what it's about: a 24-hour world-wide TV action painting with the colour turned up full." said Tony James, their mastermind, bass-player and song-writer. After founding that most commercial of punk bands, Generation X, fronted by Billy Idol, and surviving their break up in 1981, James concocted this singularly ambitious project. Taking his first page from Malcolm McLaren's book of tricks (as outlined in the *Great Rock'n'Roll Swindle*), he was inspired to create a 'scene' with his own new band at the top of the heap. Through an ad placed in *Melody Maker* and various chance run-ins on the streets of London, James vetted individuals based on their 'look' rather than their ability to play, and soon he had his dream group. Martin Degville, whose image had influenced an entire generation of New Romantics, and who proclaimed his life to be a "never-ending out-take from a John Waters movie" became the band's lead singer and spearheaded it's

burdgeoning 'video arcade fantasy' scene. "It's so much easier to teach someone to play guitar, " James said in 1988, "whereas it's impossible to teach someone charisma." After a couple of years of rehearsing, James knew what to do: "Your key man is your lawyer." he said, sounding chillingly like McLaren: "You send him in and he asks for more money and more points (dividends based on sales) than the record executive ever believed anyone would have the front to ask for." In September 1985 they got it. A strategically-placed rumour spread fast in the British media that it was four million pounds. Never before had a group without a record release won so much press, and with this first clever piece of hype, the marketing had begun. Nowhere was this more evident than in the band's stunning image. They dressed like a cross between the New York Dolls, the Beverly Hillbillies and serious fetishists, looking like technicolour PVC goth sci-fibillies behind a projected night-time image. "You see us at night-time, you think of us as futuristic and untouchable." explained James to a group of record company executives. When Sigue Sigue Sputnik's first single, 'Love Missile F1-

11' finally came out, it was unlike anything heard before in the thirty-plus year of rock'n'roll history. Their sound used gunfire, explosions and bits of Mozart, mad Thunders-esque guitar breaks, backward vocals and tons of reverb. Lines like "A US bomb cruises overhead/there goes my love rocket-red." and repeated calls to "Shoot it up!" sounded like Elvis by way of Alan Vega. With influences of Eddie Cochran, Marc Bolan, Suicide, Gene Vincent, David Bowie and Little Richard, as well as ultra-violent movies, Sigue Sigue Sputnik created the ultimate pop song. It got to No. 3 in the British charts. Their album, *Flaunt It*, opens with harsh, attention-grabbing synthesised symphonic crash, followed by a single, repeated phrase: I wanna be a star!"

This fundamentally unrestrained and honest attitude permeated every aspect of James' high concept. With the cover designed to look like the box of a Japanese action doll, *Flaunt It* was overtly packaged to appear as a product, and by flaunting the 'buy me' ethos, they also revealed a self-awareness and certain respect for the punter. They were one of the first bands to realise the sales power of an

SIGUE SIGUE SPUTNIK

"Explicit Lyrics – Parental Advisory" label (which became a permanent part of the artwork on the back cover). Openly referring to themselves as a commercial entity by using phrases like "Sputnik World Enterprises" and "A Sputnik Corporation Record", they even sold space on the jacket ("YOUR AD COULD BE HERE"). Ironically, the overtness of Sputnik's approach would have constituted the cynical marketing of a rock'n'roll group in itself, if the public hadn't felt threatened. James and co were, with a knowing wink, challenging the consumer to be manipulated, but it backfired: people took this as a challenge *not* to be manipulated, and despite enormous fame in England, they didn't really take off. Their crassness did, however, gain Sputnik a cult following in America that consisted of bored, suburban teenagers.

The technique of 'cutting through the crap' is now a regular concept for advertising agencies in their attempts to court jaded twenty-somethings. 'This is an ad, we want you to buy this' they say. As always though, the progenitors do it with panache, of which Sputnik had more than enough. In the end, all that's left if *Flaunt It*, one entertaining album (well they did release one more studio album, *Dress for Excess* in 1988, but that's not worth mentioning at all). But it's Tony James who deserves the final say on his creation. Buried within *Flaunt It*'s inner sleeve collage is James' last word on the matter: "PS: a sense of humour is always essential."

Bart Bealmear

Until less than a hundred years ago, women copied men's men's styles above but not below the waist. The fashion in modesty allowed men only to show they they had two separate legs. Women had to conceal the fact; also that they had two buttocks and, at one time, even their ankles.

This curious standard of decency was challenged in 1849 by Mrs Amelia Jenks Bloomer of Seneca Falls, new York. She put her name into the English language by designing for American women a pair of baggy trousers similar to those worn by Turkish men.

THE LOUIS VELVETEEN. NOTE WELL !

The word "LOUIS" in connection with this Velveteen is spelled "L·O·U·I·S," AND IS NO OTHER WAY.

LE FOLLET :

The "LOUIS" VELVETEEN, though draping with the rich folds of linen velvet—which the subtle shadows and beautiful " bloom" cause is exactly sensibly—is infinitely lighter in cost. It possesses, also, an incalculable advantage, which even alone would account for the favour it receives from those who understand the ART of DRESS, viz., by a particular method of looking the pile, this resists any injury from creasing, dust, or even rain, and preserves the freshness of its appearance to the last day of its wear.

THE "LOUIS" VELVETEEN IS SOLD BY

Decency

a drill — strong twilled linen

corset in scarlet drill and cage crinoline

MRS AMELIA BLOOMER

LORGNETTE A PAIR OF SPECTACLES ATTATCHED TO A HANDLE AT ONE SIDE

day of its wear.

THE "LOUIS" VELVETEEN IS SOLD BY ALL DRAPERS THROUGHOUT THE KINGDOM.

on the most GUARANTEED

A dedication to PL Travers' grand-daughters

Kitty Lindy

Cicily Jane

It's raining Mary Poppins!

dorothy's into death

Budget Suave

Button Down

The shirt is perfect; it's been wailing like a synthetic siren from the clothes-rail, urging you to dash yourself on its Rayon rockface. It's the right colour, the right fit but the collars redefine fly-away. 180 degree monstrosities that even the most hardened swinger would find difficult to live with. The answer is simple, button down. Tuck the offending tips behind your collar-bone and you can mark where the necessary sartorial incisions should be made. Lash out your two quid and get down the market. Find the button stall and purchase three (the same size as the shirt's originals, in my experience finding any smaller is an exercise in plastic futility), next, take the shirt down the tailors (Franco, 47 Carnaby Street, is perfect for these alterations) or dry cleaners. For three pounds he'll cut the holes and sew on the buttons (two on the front, one at the back) and voila: for under a tenner you are now the proud owner of an unique garment that you won't find at The Dispensary. Rule of thumb: the wider the flare, the higher the collar when pinned back, so it's easy to transform the most acrylic of eye-sores into a swinging John Stephens number.

My Soul is a Safari-Suit

Develop a beige mind. Most Charity hangers are awash with cheap off-cream garments to put aside palpitating visions of OAP bus rides and crap easy listening clubs, instead think Alain Delon in Paris (M&S three quarter length, three button mac), Bobby De Niro's Florida menace, circa Goodfellas (Keynote safari shirt with vicious epaulettes) or sporty Harry Palmer (early 80s St Michael golfing jacket). On the whole, they tend to show up less grime than their white counterparts and even the occasional stain lends an air of park-bench sleaze. Most can be washed on a non-fast coloured cycle, thus skirting the dry-cleaners, and are the perfect attire for impressing your fiancee's parents.

Andrew Cop

THE UNFASHIONABLE OPINIONS OF
WICKED WILLIE

WHEN YOU READ THIS YOU'LL probably think "what a prick". Well that's OK – I am a prick.

Since time began, or at least, when I first appeared in human form, I have been introduced to and into countless women – a fact which you have to admit, entitles me to know what of I am talking.

Don't worry, this isn't going to be a 'women through the ages' but I thought I should start by establishing my credentials. What's clear to me is that men haven't changed – we are simply cave dwellers in suits and after-shave.

But girls have changed. In fact you change what you wear, what you eat, what you think and your knickers on what seems to be a daily basis.

The motivation for all this is one of the most abominable words in the dictionary:

FASHION

Fashion is only a bunch of manipulators pointing the way ahead to the gullible, while making strange utterances, such as 'red is the new blue' and 'hemlines are down an inch and a half' and 'you're nobody without a v.p.l.'

Even some men are fashion victims, but I really don't want to talk about them.

Anyway, since the Fur Age, girls started wearing high heels and dresses, and today, on the whole, look a lot foxier than they did in the days when dinner parties were sitting round the fire, eating the tribe next door.

As a willie, what I like in women is anything that gives me a reading – makes my needle flicker so to speak. Let's start with bottoms…

Perfect – keep it up with the pasta

Bottoms.

I do like a girl with a nice fat bum – not too fat you understand – but substantial. A perfect bottom is also nice, but the competition for those is very stiff, and because of the supply and demand factor, they tend to be high maintenance.

Bony assed women are just not on – so please stop working out – it won't work even if it works. If never comes off your butt anyway, thank god.

Nice shoes, and the right way up..

Underwear

'No bra' is best if you can get away with it, and it's still pretty interesting if you can't.

for the last decade and a half girls have been conned into believing that high sided knickers and bikinis make the legs look longer. They don't. They make legs look shorter and the effect is far from erotic. Thank god big knickers and straight across panties are back in favour.

Needless to say I hate tights. They look ugly and they're a hassle to get off. There's no excuse for them. Hold ups look good, but I've heard they can strangle your legs. For me stockings and suspenders are the difference between pink and purple.

Shoes

OK, strappy high heeled sandals please. Simple high heeled shoes are nice or casual, low sided sneakers or old fashioned plimmies. Boots are sexy if they're ankle length. I can't stand knee length boots, and boots that go over the knee make you look like a sixties hooker – horrible! As are platforms – they make feet look clumpy and legs skinny. Men's shoes, ugh! Trainers, Yeaach! Don't do it. Ever. And don't tell me you can't walk in stilettos – you only have to point them at the ceiling and kick them off when you get out of bed.

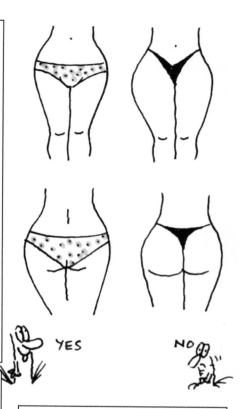

YES   NO

Hair

To have a short hairstyle a girl has to be very pretty, or ugly enough for it not to matter anyway.

HOW LONG HAIR CAN
IMPROVE THE LOOKS

Check out this tattoo!

Jewellery

Jewellery is great if it makes you look tarty, and that doesn't mean expensive. Willies are not impressed by women festooned in diamonds and gold bangles – it just looks vulgar. All you need are some diamante earrings, some delicate little chains and bracelet and maybe a fine ankle chain just to make us extra hard.

So remember – tarty, not vulgar if you can get your head round that concept. Tattoos are also OK if the same rule is followed.

Dunno about body piercing. Clitty rings are OK if they're big enough to attach a dog lead to, but nasal, naval and eyebrow piercing is not very becoming on a grown-up woman. And nose studs simply look like snot, but if that's what you want good luck.

Body Hair

The Americans have always insisted that women shave their underarm hair and have a bikini wax. It is totally unnecessary and quite unattractive. French, German and most European women just let it grow, and are of course more sexy. British girls should rebel and say not to the wax and the shave. Well, OK – maybe the legs then but that's all. That's all.

I need a bikini wax

Don't do it!

Budget Suave

Dig the Dry-Cleaners

The first thing to remember is that Dry Cleaners are for everyone. Don't be put off by Granddad connotations or the appalling vision of bankers picking up candy-striped double-cuffs, these houses of hygiene offer a myriad of other services to fit even the most meagre of resources. For instance, skirt the hell of ironing by getting tops and trousers pressed. I've hand the razor-sharp creases in classic Wrangler cords re-established for as little as £3.20 in Brixton and, of course, there's nothing quite like that feeling of pride as you swagger homeward, freshly sterilised fabric slung over your shoulder, old fashioned metal hanger biting into fingers, clear plastic garment bag trailing.

Rocker Bye BAY-be BAD!

In defence of OLD BANGERS

as all drivers of crap old cars will admit, motoring pleasure comes from dubious circumstances. Not for us the thrill of sheer horsepower, joys of fluid handling or even the ego-boost of admiring glances down the high street; no, the best buzz is seeing cars younger than yours stranded by the roadside. I was struggling up a protracted incline in my 16-year-old Fiesta one afternoon, with a Talbot

Samba behind me, when we passed a new BMW 5-series – in the lay-by, with bonnet up and AA van in attendance. In my rear-view mirror, I saw the Samba driver and his passenger pointing with glee at the B-M and laughing their heads off.

Such pleasures are rare; when you run a sub-£500 car, you inhabit the strange hinterland where it is no longer a respectably practical concern, but not (yet) a classic or cult vehicle. exempt from the pressures of keeping up with the

neighbours, having the latest, trendiest metallic paint finish or gadget/gizmo, fads and fashions in motoring pass you by. 4x4 jeeps? People-carriers? The latest tiny town cars? Nothing to do with me, guv. However, you also miss out on the camaraderie of cult/classic car owners, the rallies and owner's clubs, the waves from drivers of the same model. In effect, we are virtually invisible and completely anonymous.

Running an elderly Fiesta, Metro, Fiat Panda or similar has none of the rewards of, say, a Beetle, or 2CV, which inspire passionate defences. There isn't even the so-crap-it's cool factor of the Austin Allegro, Princess, Maxi or other examples of British Leyland's finest moments. The obvious question is Why? and the obvious answer is Cost.

Less obvious is the bloody-minded sense of pride in keeping an old banger going, or completing a mammoth expedition. In its very crudity, the involvement and engagement in the driving

Photographs: Farah AlKalisi

SAP 171X

process denied to the driver of the slick modern cocoon-car: the stubborn refusal to conform to fashions, by into status symbols, or indeed, make a style statement of any kind, or even a desperate (or misguided) last stand against the nanny state, which decrees we must have air-bags, side-impact bars, seatbelt pretensioners and crumple zones, eat 5 portions of vegetables a day, sleep 7 hours a night and wipe our bottoms front-to-back.

I could walk into a showroom tomorrow, and leave behind the wheel of a new Corsa, Clio, or even a Golf, if I was prepared to sign away my independence for the finance agreement. So, if you ever see me standing in the rain on a hard-shoulder, spare me your sympathy; I'm not pathetic, just perverse. But could you give me a push?

Farah AlKalisi

The Worst Old Bangers of all

(10) Chrysler/Talbot Horizon: Conceived at the fag-end of the Chrysler/Talbot Sunbeam buy-ups, hastily killed off when Peugeot swallowed the whole lot up.

(9) Vauxhall Chevette: The UK version of General Motors' first "world car". Pity the rest of the world who bought it too.

(8) Daf (anything)**:** Holland's contribution to vehicle technology was an early CVT automatic system, the Variomatic, which made an otherwise cheap and cheerful little car drive like a mild float.

(7) Datsun/Nissan Sunny: Brought Japanese technology to the masses. Many wondered how a car managed to be so cheap and nasty, yet also so bloody durable.

(6) Hyundai Pony: And this one paved the way for even cheaper and even nastier Far Eastern imports.

(5) Seat Ibiza (-93)**:** Before the VW takeover, Seat make recycled Fiats. They didn't even use the best bits, and tried to redeem the Ibiza by using engines made from the Porsche parts bin. Possibly the worst attempt to polish a turd ever.

(4) Austin Maestro: And speaking of turds... the Maestro came in strangely popular shades of brown and beige. It says a lot about why the British motor industry went into terminal decline.

(3) Renault Fuego: Renault's attempt at a rival to the Ford Capri and VW Sirocco. Yeah, right. This was no sports car, and nobody bought one. Except my mother.

(2) Volvo 340: The spare bits left over when Volvo bought Daf (see above). Smug people buy it thinking they're getting an especially safe old car. They're not. It's not a proper Volvo.

(1) Ford Fiesta: Truly democratic motoring. Cheap to buy and run, even for doleys, single parents, student and everyone generally priced out of useful participation in cunsumer society. Through a funny quirk of bureaucracy, the 957cc ones qualify for the £100 'green' car tax, even though their ancient, feeble engines pump out enough pollutants to give whole nursery schools asthma. Buy one and piss off John Prescott, your snobbish neighbours and tree-huggers. Biased. Of course I am. Marvellous.

ENOUGH!

STYLE: Manner of doing. Distinctive manner of person. Quality or manner. Fashion in dress etc.

FASHION: Prevailing custom or style, esp. in dress . In fashion: Conforming with current usage.

Like it or not, we consume too much, 20% of the world's population consume 80% of its resources, produce over 60% of its greenhouse gas emissions and are responsible for over 75% of toxic waste.

Whoops. This means we're going to have to do something about it, get environmental and consume less. Fair enough, but does this mean we all have to dress like one of those people who come along and have an inspiring talk that you totally agree with about what needs to be changed in the world, but somehow look like their mother chose their clothes? Uh-uh, not in the least.

Just because we're not addicted to shopping for new threads every Saturday doesn't mean we can't look absolutely gorgeous. Some politicos think that taking more than two seconds to choose your outfit for the day means that you're shallow, but they haven't got a clue when it comes to the inexplicable and fundamental importance of style, they just don't understand.

As every *Cheap Date* reader knows, it's pathetically easy to look fabulous with jumble sale finds and a bit of imagination. Taking pleasure in how things look isn't the same as being completely obsessed with appearances. Being aware that we share responsibility for many of the world's problems isn't the same as being a badly dressed, hairshirty, earnest, worthy-smelling drongo. A world that pleasures your senses is entirely compatible with a world that doesn't over consume; there's no conflict between the two possibilities.

And let's not confuse fashion with style – style is an expression of individuality and, despite what advertisers try to tell you, following fashion isn't. You don't become more individual by buying a product heavily marketed with this decade's favourite Unique Selling Point: Individuality. For all that, the fashion industry has its share of maverick geniuses and people who are passionate about clothes, but for the most part it's run by businessmen who are more interested in the bottom line than the A line, and who know that their profits depend on people thinking that clothes they bought three months ago are already boring.

Enough said.

Jane Lawson and Paul Fitzgerald
ENOUGH – Anti Consumerism
Campaign and organisers of
National No Shop Day.

August 14th, 1920
by
Lorna Miller

Look Your Best at the Sea

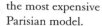

A bathing cap, however becoming, would suit no one, however classical her features, if worn like the picture at left. But pulled down well over the forehead, with a few stray wisps of hair artfully arranged at the sides, as in the lower picture, it would prove a more fascinating head-dress than the most expensive Parisian model.

"There's nothing I love so much as 'lazing' on the sea front!" said this little maiden. Certainly, if correctly done, you must admit it makes a charming picture! Be careful though to get your sunshade at just the right angle, your hands not too close together, and arrange your feet so as to strike a straight line from the shoulder. After that you may "laze" to your heart's content, quite satisfied that you look the picture of health and beauty.

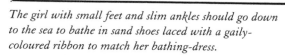

The girl with small feet and slim ankles should go down to the sea to bathe in sand shoes laced with a gaily-coloured ribbon to match her bathing-dress.

The Complexion

It is quite impossible to prevent the face from getting wet, even if the head is not dipped, so the best plan is just to rub a little vaseline or a simple cream all over the face and neck. It's wonderful how this simple precaution spares the complexion.

The Hair

The opportunity to let the hair hang loose for as long as possible must be taken advantage of. It is a good excuse to give the hair a real sun bath, the best tonic it can have. Be careful, however, not to get the hair wet when bathing to avoid the "drowned rat" look!

CB Radio

Citizens Band Radio (CB) became a huge craze in the US in 1976, and by the time it reached these shores the boom there was all but finished. The CB was the Internet, a mobile phone and bleeper all rolled into one in that 70s chunky-dialled way.

Initially a way for truckers to keep up to date with traffic problems and keep an eye out for Smokey Bears (police) enforcing the meagre double nickels (55 mph) speed limit in the US, the CB was given mass appeal by films such as *Convoy* (it's plot lifted from the eponymous hit single by CW McCall) and the imaginatively titled *Citizens Band* (early Johnathan Demme film using CB as a metaphor for lack of human communication). There was even *CB Mamas* – a CB based porn flick.

CB was a walkie-talkie for your car or home that allowed you to communicate over the airwaves and converse with your "good buddies". Range and reception

Know your Geography!

London	Smoke City
Birmingham	Dead City
Bolton	Chip Butty Town
Glasgow	Second City
Horley	Night City
Liverpool	Murky River City
Manchester	Rainy City
Norwich	Canary Town
Portsmouth	Booze City
Bridgewater	Smelly Town
Belfast	Soul City
Luton	Dreamy Town
Sleaford	Customville
Croydon	Big City

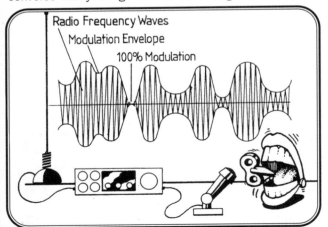

Radio Frequency Waves
Modulation Envelope
100% Modulation

varied according to your rig (radio) and your twig (aerial) as well as a host of other anorak-friendly add-ons and extras. There was also the outlaw aspect – AM transmission was allegedly best, but it was FM that was made legal in the UK in 1981. This lead to AM users seeing themselves as *Dukes of Hazzard*-type outlaws – aware that Buzby (the GPO as it was) could come for them at any time. The real CB enthusiast knew that the state found them far more threatening than the IRA or even communism.

There followed a rash of spin-off musical abominations by country artists such as Merle Haggard. There was even a UK top ten hit by Red Sovine. Many

CB Speak – It's Easy!

Base twenty:
Operator's home
Bean Store:
Restaurant
Blacktop: Major road
Bra Buster:
Lady with huge norks
Breaker: CB user
Bubble Trouble:
A tyre problem
Go Juice: Fuel
Keep the shiny side up and the greasy side down:
Have a safe trip
Negatory: No
Permanently 10-7:
Dead
Preganant Roller Skate: VW Beetle
Rig/Squawk Box: CB set
Road Tar: Coffee
Shake the trees and rake the leaves:
Vehicle at the rear and front of a convoy watching out for police
Snafu: Cock-up
Ten-Four: Yes

Ten-Four Hundred:
Drop dead
Twenty: Location

There is an official "10" code used with meanings from 10-0 to 10-99 that are slightly different in America and a disappearing "Q" code (3 letters beginning with Q). Then there is the "13" insult code, which everybody knows:

13-1: You're an idiot
13-2: I'm ignoring you
13-3: You're beautiful when you're angry
13-4: Sorry
13-20: Is your mike clicking or are your uppers loose again?
13-22: Is that your voice or did you install a steam whistle?
13-26: Next time you eat garlic speak further from the mike!

were based on the CB language that was all in code and numbers – much of which seemed to be different terms for women (Seatcovers). Yes, the CB world was inhabited by far too many middle aged roll-up smoking men in cardigans who believed they had a way with the ladies.

There is still a hardcore of CB users, but it has not gained any kind of retro cool in recent years. But you may want to grab a rig at the boot sale – just in case Tarantino's next film is a re-make of *Smokey and the Bandit*.

Iain Aitch

Anita Pallenberg

Cheap Date interviews the most stylish person it can think of.

Anita: I've got this friend of mine, he says "What do you do all afternoon?" and I say: "Oh I go to the gym." and he doesn't know, I hate the tell him because its a bit like taking drugs and drinking, or the fucking cigarettes. I roam around second hand shops and get off on the fact that I can find something cheap. For me it's not that I feel guilty, but I know about compulsions and things from drugs, so I do know that thing of shopping is just as bad. As far as I'm concerned, it's better than putting needles in your arm or stuff up your nose, but it is part of the same thing — the same area of the brain. Whenever I get the compulsion to make myself feel better, I always go to a second hand shop, but

it comes in waves. There was a period when I used to return my clothes and do the whole exchange bit but I haven't done that for years. I've really got to empty my cupboard.

God, I'd love to be there.

I've got nothing left from the 60s. Everybody always asks me "You must have tons of stuff." but we had a couple of fires so I lost everything — it was heartbreaking. there was an auction in Los Angeles and all the actresses sold all their stuff. I got a fox fur coat that used to belong to Joan Crawford — a beigey, creamy kind of white, massive shoulders, really tight. That one I lost in a fire. I had another little fox vest which I gave away — I've given so much stuff away. And people are always nicking my stuff. They think because I've got so many clothes that I won't notice. maybe not on the same day, but I always notice. I've had that so much you know. I've got totally trashy stuff, and real nice stuff which I get from different kinds of second hand shops. I don't really go for labels but I do have an old Pucci. That one I'm not going to throw out, and then I've got all the Vivienne Westwood. Those I just keep.

Have you got any of the collectable punk stuff?

In the punk period I was living in Switzerland, more into ski-ing.

Are you any good at finding things?

Yeah, I've got this friend in New York — a designer called Anna Sui, and she had this beautiful crushed velvet Victorian-style jacket that I really wanted. It was like $500, and I said "I'm gonna find one just the same in a second hand shop." I found one for $30 — it took me a while, but I had this mania that I get when I see something I must have. It takes time though. I must say I do waste a lot of time at these shops. Usually it's just my little secret. Yesterday I went out at 2pm and at 5 I was still in that fucking shop (Steinberg and Tolkein in London), rummaging and talking. It's part of my thing. I've done design work and I've always been interested in fashion, so rummaging for second-hand clothes is my inspiration.

Your own form of art?

Yeah yeah (HA HA). Artisans in the old days like Fortuni, the way he did pleats in a way that nobody else knew how, is fascinating. I take Marc Jacobs

to Portobello Market and we can discuss the details of seams and button holes for hours. I've studies costumes from the Greeks to the Egyptians, everything. All this stuff from the 60s and 70s now is a bit daunting because I've been through it once – you do see people dressing the way I dressed in the 60s. It might be me looking at it subjectively but I don't think the revival looks the same: the fabrics, buttons, seams and hems are totally

different. It's not good enough for me, but I guess you've got to live with it. For me the bias cut from the 30s is much more important and valid than A-line and Mary Quant and all that stuff. There was one good designer in the 60s called Rudy Gernrech – American. He did the topless bathing suits with two straps, but mostly knitwear. I haven't got anything of his – you don't really see it apart from sometimes in New York.

Can you pinpoint how you got your style?

I just think it's an expression of myself. Clothes have been a passion that I've had for as long as I can remember. My mum had great style, and this beautiful trunk full of clothes that she got rid of without telling me – it really upset me. All this fabulous lamé stuff. And I

had this aunt who was not exactly eccentric, but she always wore gorgeous stuff and looked beautiful. She made herself look better with the clothes.

What do you tend to like?

I go through phases – bags, hats… I love jewellery, though it's more difficult to know these days with such good fakes. I'm a total sucker for anything that looks shiny. Shoes have always been my fetish, but that's another Italian kind of thing. I've got lots of 40s shoes, though I'm now into stilettos which isn't very good because I ride a bike. Whatever style it is, if I admire it, I'll wear it. At the moment I'm looking out for that 50s/60s fabric – heavy Chantel, and always cashmere which I get from Portobello. I go through taste phases as well, but when I start to see other people wearing the same thing instead of saying "Oh great, now I'm in on it," I just go the other way round. I like it when people compliment what I'm wearing. maybe it's the desire to feel special and different, which I always had anyway, so it comes out in clothes.

Meanwhile Jett and his mates were trying to have a stag night out at Zenith

Shit, it's closed

His friends look so cool because they're in rockin' London band THE CHEETAHS

Uh-Huh

Oh well, I'll have a fag. Thanks...

And get really drunk!

Due to their immensely fun and debauched revelry, they didn't see Kenneth, approaching Zenith...

Jett Blak! You stay away from my sister and Zenith. It's my favourite nightclub.

Aw shit it's closed!

Putney can do what she wants...

And she wants a bit of THIS!!

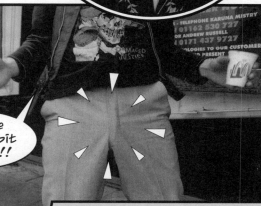

Oh dear, he's said it now...

RAAAAAHHHHHHHGGGGGGG!!!!!!!!!!

Steady on mate

To the secret, pre-appointed venue he ran...

We'll deal with him. You hurry to your waiting bride

... nervous about taking the responsibility of life as a marital unit, but keeping it all under control.

The Wedding Guests arrive...

← Nigel Kennedy's legs!

continued on page 124

Cute!

I have always dreamed of finding a Moog or Theramin synthesiser at a car-boot-sale or in a junk shop. As someone with no musical talent whatsoever, the idea of a device that can make a great selection of beeps and drones with little effort is very appealing.

So far this has remained just a thrift fantasy, but last Autumn in Queens Park I did make the most amazing find at the now-defunct Carlton Vale boot sale.

I was flicking through a box of records with a surprisingly large Partridge Family content when I spied something interesting out of the corner of my eye. It was half-buried under a mound of battered tape decks and unidentified circuit boards.

It was clear from the distinctive keyboard that it was Rolf Harris' second favourite instrument, a Stylophone. But this was not a mere white, flimsy plastic hand-held model, the sort that retro collector shops turn up fairly often. This was the Über stylophone, the king of high-pitched vibration. If the Queen had ever played *House of the Rising Sun* on a Stylophone, then this is the model that she would have used.

I picked it up and looked it over, summoned all my high tech know-how and asked, " Excuse me mate, does this work?" The stallholder replied that it did, in a tone that suggested: "Don't fucking know, don't fucking care." But at three quid it was well worth the gamble.

The machine is just over a foot wide, just under a foot long and three inches deep. It has 26 keys on its metal keyboard, and most importantly it has two styli. You can play with both at once, creating crazy mixtures of noise from both ends of the keyboard. One stylus is your normal bleep, single tone job. But the other is what lends this model, the 350S, its special status.

The second stylus is for re-iteration. That is, it produces a continually pulsing tone for which you have a choice of two speeds. So what you get is a di-di-di-di-di-di-di-di noise reminiscent of *The Flight of the Bumblebee*.

The fun doesn't end there either. The huge clunking plastic switches on the top of the beast give you a vast array of other noises to play with too. There is a wah-wah, a vibrato function with a choice of ferocity and two decay options. You can choose your noise from the selection of woodwind or string instruments, mixing the two sounds to your own desired effect. The sound of a 30 piece wah-wah string band with vibrating re-iteration is truly an electronic surf sensation.

I don't remember ever seeing any advertising for this product in the 70s, whereas I do remember the ads with Rolf for the normal Stylophone. Maybe this model was advertised with a family scene: children gathered round, beautiful music flowing from what you thought was a grand piano, but when the camera zoomed, it revealed that the sounds actually came from the sophisticated 350S.

My favourite theory is that very few of them were ever made and that this was a prototype given to the likes of Mancini and Baccarach to compose with. Maybe Kraftwerk were offered one too but didn't understand the instructions on this English product. If only Casio hadn't come along and taken over the market with its insidious Vialtone then the modern dancefloor might now be a very different place.

Iain Aitch

The Shnorer

Hello shnorers everywhere. This piece of low-rent writing is designed to help you, the honourable Cheap Dater, in case you ever find yourself catapulted through a temporal gateway into the Jewish East End of 1910, like the chap in the green turtle-neck jumper in *The Time Tunnel*.

Here in Brick Lane in the old days you'll be able to carry out your noble thrifty lifestyle, but you'll need to stay on your toes and carry about three cubic tons of emergency reserve *chutzpah* in your back pocket.

Imagine the scene in that Edwardian ghetto. I'm afraid you'll have to imagine, a my descriptive powers aren't sufficient to generate emotive visual imagery. Thing of people bustling around in black and white talking about stuff and wearing hats of all shapes and sizes as long as they're identical trilbys. You want me to do everything for you? I'm not Don DeLillo and you couldn't afford him anyway. It was you who bought this Value For Money publication rather than forking out on some expensive novel in fancy-schmancy hardback that gives you a hernia every time you lift it.
So stop complaining.

Anyway, let's all calm down as I sweat blood trying to offer you a glossary of terms from the hard-bitten magic of the old Yiddish ghetto, while you just sit back and read in your comfy chair, unaware or perhaps even uncaring of the pain and anguish that I have to go through writing this stuff. Enjoy!

Shnorer (rhymes with horror)
Had *Cheap Date* been published amongst the old Jewish community, it would most surely have been called The *Shnorer*. *Shnorers* were originally beggars who saw themselves as on a mission for God. The classic *shnorer* would suggest that he was doing you a favour by taking your money. Jewish law demands alms giving and without the *shnorer's* selfless assistance you'd be in big trouble – a fact which he never let you forget.

In latter years, *shnoring* evokes a guilt-free life of freeloading and obsessive bargain-hunting that I believe will be familiar to many of you. But the true *shnorer* is still distinguished from the tun of the mill bargain-hunter by their sincerely held belief that it is his or her divine right to get maximum value at all times. For the real *shnorer* morality, reality, logic, economics and law are but paper curtains to the torn aside in the dogged spiritual pursuit of the ultimate freebie or bargain.

Chutzpah (pronounced like a Mancurian would say 'huts' with a Welsh 'll' as in Llandudno at the front. And 'pah' is pronounced 'per'. Easy.) You'll need plenty of this elegant combination of cheek, charm and sheer effrontery if you're to make it as a truly great shnorer. There was lots of *chutzpah* in the old East End. It was virtually a prerequisite for survival. So you'd find shops with front signage hung upside down or spelt wrong so that people would come into their shop to tell them about it, thus becoming potential consumers. In later times, Malcolm McClaren turned post-situationalist art *chutzpah* into punk, but that's another story.

Gelt
Never let too much *gelt* (money) get in the way of your *shnoring* activities. All the best shnorers in the old days were well dressed and capable of charm (all the better to *shnor* with) – but poverty is nothing to be ashamed

(a Yiddish Glossary)

of, as in the cheery sign above the Pawn Brokers:

Come In!
Don't Be Shy!
Borrow You Way Out of Debt!

K'Naker (Kerr, as in Graham Kerr the Galloping Gourmet, and Nucker, which rhymes with Tucker.)
The *K'Naker* is a Yiddish Big Cheese, a boss–figure or similar fellow of stature, and represents a dream goal for every shnorer. It is said that within every shnorers there's a *K'Naker*. Use of this term is recommended in all shops where you're not getting consumer satisfaction. Sigh a world-weary sign at the assistant and ask to see the *K'Naker*. That'll put them in their place.

Shlock

Shoddy, cheap rubbish that no self-respecting shnorer should ever accept.

Gonef (Don if)

Literally a thief, but by association someone who has lots of *chutzpah* and not so much *gelt*. Someone who lives by his wits, or a cheeky child that always gets his or her way through charm and guile. Bart Simpson is a *gonef* in this respect. The *gonef shnorer* can charm his or her way to complete consumer satisfaction while never having to pay retail prices.

Luftmensch (put bench)

God forbid that you're ever taken for *luftmensch* – because a *luftmensch* is a sucker, a patsy, the eternal drawer of the short straw who nevertheless dreams of power and wealth and respect, and while he's doing this dreaming, the *Shnorers* and *Gonefs* rise to be *K'Nakers*. The *luftmensch* is a *shmendrick*, by any other name.

Trettverten

This is nothing to do with anything, but I'm trying to propagate use of this very useful word. These are the 'step words', those words which you always think of on the steps as you leave someone's house, those sparkly bon mots that would have been a really witty riposte to something someone said to you previously, but occur only as cruel *trettverten* at which point they're not good to anybody. A useful word, I hope you'll agree, especially for those of us whose social like consists entirely of such *trettverten*.

Greg Rowlands

the smoking suit

don't put your daughter on the stage mrs.Worthington

YOU'RE A GOOD SPORT WHEN YOU DRESS FOR IT...

mad money 'stays put' in this pleated Acetate Crepe bag with 'jools' on top with the right fixin's inside

A GALLANT YOUNG SWAGGER COAT IN ONE OF THE GLORIOUS NEW SHADOW PLAID COATINGS

GET THAT SUMMER TAN IN TRUNKS

SWING SMART

Style THE MOST DRAMATIC

FROM A... ...OAT

YOU'RE A GOOD SPORT WHEN YOU DRESS FOR IT...

Blow 'em Away Nesta!

THE COAT AND THE CANADIAN WHO LOVED IT

On a drizzly Friday afternoon in early October, the Year of Our Thrifty Lord Nineteen Hundred and Ninety-Eight, a certain gentleman-about-town named Bum (a.k.a. Greg Harris, but you're not supposed to know that) began a breathtaking revolution in high-end thrift. He is a splendid dresser every day, with a taste for accessories like rose-colored sunglasses and faux ivory cigarette holders. And he likes the vintage threads, big-time. We all know there's funky clothes to be found on the cheap; then there's funky clothes for FREE. This is what Bum began, and one man's Quest for the Greatest Coat of All TIME is a tale to inspire Cheapos everywhere.

Here's how it went down: on that special Friday, Bum was cruising and perusing the streets of Downtown with his friend Tarka Cordell, who casually suggested a visit to the shop Resurrection, on Mott Street. A renowned thrifter and clotheshorse I his own right, Cordell immediately made eye contact with the store's' crown jewel – a coat – and had a rush of emotion we have all experience one time or another: I MUST HAVE IT!! He tried it on. Disaster. Tarka has the

shoulders of an Olympic swimmer, and the coat simply could not accommodate them. Chagrined, he offered the coat to Bum.

An then… Pure Magic. This moment cannot be overemphasised – it is every thrifter's duty and joy to pass on clothes that don't fit, and all of New York agrees that Tarka and Bum are together in an elite class of dressers. To survive, they most cooperate (think Russia and China sharing nuclear secrets). Tarka had just one stipulation: "I, and I alone am responsible." he said, levying his tax, "one in five chicks the Coat pulls is mine."

To be blunt, no coat has ever belonged on any one person like this Robert Warner doeskin/leopard coat belongs on Bum, and that's a real not to Bum. To hell with Joseph and his fucking Technicolor Dreamcoat – try chocolate-coloured doeskin with REAL leopard-fur cuffs and collar. Brass buttons with Indian heads run down the front, and the stitching is done with thick leather cords. Quite simply, amazing. Also quite amazing, the price. Nobody panicked when they saw the numbers. $1000.00. That's a lot of bread. No thrifter in their right mind should spend that, but

Photograph: Nigel mogg

passing up the coat was simply unthinkable. So he did the right thing: he asked the store's comely and copacetic proprietors Katy ad Megan if he could put down a small deposit to hold the coat, and this was born the Bum Coat Fund.

In the Tennessee Williams classic, *A Streetcar Named Desire*, Blanche Dubois proudly exclaims, "I have always relied upon the kindness of strangers." Taking this philosophy to heart, Bum did the following: he took a Polaroid of the coat, and taped it to an empty Maraschino Cherry jar, and placed the jar on the bar at the heinously faded and jaded nightspot Wax, where he was bartending at the time. He and his friend Molly threw in a couple of bucks, "to kind of get things rolling." Lo and behold, It Began. New Yorkers can be perversely generous at times, and the love between a boy and his coat was obvious. Before long, the Bum Coat Fund had amassed several hundred dollars. Bit-by-bit (or stitch-by-stitch), his regular instalments and lengthy visitations continued. "I don't know what will happen once he takes that coat," says Megan, "it's brought a lot of people into the store. They just want to check out that famous coat." Added Katy, "The designer in LA heard about all of this and says he's going to start a Corvette fund." Well, Mr Warner, that really all depends upon how you look in a Corvette...

It gives this reporter great pleasure to inform you that by press time, the Bum Coat Fund now stands at approximately $870 (Bum's currently tending bar at SWAY, nightlife impresario Nur Kahn's teeming den of pleasure on the western reaches of Spring Street.) He's excited to be so

close to his goal. His Quest has become a cause celebre in his hometown of Oshowa, Ontario, and there's even talk of it Uptown. You may have heard about the clothes making the man, but this is a heartwarming fable about the man

making the means to make the clothes. Remember, if it's the right garment, ANYTHING is possible for the creatively dedicated thrifter.

Bum and the Coat. The Coat and Bum. May they live happily ever after.

Alex Freidman

Budget Suave

The Market Stall Holder is My Friend

Locate the nearest street market in your area. Avoid the knocked-off hi-fi equipment and second-hand records, which on the whole tend only to be warped copies of Peters & Lee atrocities, instead head for the arrangement of mirrors, deck-chairs and clothes-rails which immediately denote the groovy-clobber merchant. Make contact with an informal greeting such as "alright mate?" (Note: this works for both sexes) then assume the guise of cloth connoisseur as you browse, "umming" and "ahhing" betwixt the hangers.

By now the stall holder is intrigued. Maximise your hypnotic potential by making spurious yet assured comments i.e. "This shirt can't be '67 can it? 'Cos the back-pleat's too narrow and anyway they only added J-Tex collars round '69 which was quite late really and..." The stall-holder is impressed, so get on first name terms. Chat about where they get the stuff, how long they've had their pitch and how you admire the small hip business person.

Offer them a smoke if you've got any, drop in how skint you are and can't afford the tenner price-tag and offer them seven. Invariably they'll take pity (especially if they're a trifle zonked).

Happily tell them to "Take it easy man," and that you'll "Check 'em next week", then invest the change in your favourite juicer.

Andrew Copeman

MARC BOLAN

Marc Bolan WAS A wizard. Literally, metaphorically, whatever. Creativity is a magical process – if it's not, it's carpentry to me. Music is the highest form of creativity/art/magic and Marc was a uniquely, totally creative person, a kind of magical conduit able to express his whole personality with perfect clarity through his music, lyrics, singing, guitar playing, his body… everything. The only other guitar player I like as much is James Williamson, someone else who recorded almost nothing but masterpieces. Marc is my favorite lyricist too, though most people will tell you he sang nothing but gibberish. I love what he did. He really made it all up himself, bursting the veil of logic to reach a far more interesting – and profound – parallel universe of his own devising. He was his own start point. If he drew on the work of others at all, his vision transfigured his sources. This is the mark of a true artist, a true magician.

Text and comic détournage: Rob Coyne • Executed by: Eugene Coyne & Tim Lambert

I'm like a child in the sand on the beach of the land of you/My life's a shadowless horse if I can't get across to you

Soul of My Suit

Mark Palmer remembers a few things about his friend Marc Bolan and his green suit.

E JUST SAID "DO YOU WANT that" I said "Yeaeaaher!" I lived at Cwm-Yr-Erthin and he came and stayed with me... Marc and I were very close, he was an exceptionally nice guy... I knew some of his mates in the hippie days, he was Penny Guinness' lodger in Little Venice... I was a fan of his music before I met him... Saw him and Peregrin Took at the Royal Albert Hall supporting Donovan. I thought it was pretty far out for his time... He was sharp, funny, clever, nice, quite an exceptional poet... very canny, a wise kid... Bits of paper he'd written down rhymes everywhere... I went out one evening with Penny and met him and we became good friends just like that... Mickey Finn became a friend too... Marc bought a conventional country house near Ross-on-Wye... I sold him a wee spotted pony called Spotted Dick and put him there, and another one to keep it company.

He was with Gloria when he died... I didn't know him then. By that time the wheels of the rock world were spinning and taking over.

The suit was a Mr Freedom – Tommy Robertson.

Lord of the Rings was the epic of the age... he was just like something out of *Lord of the Rings*. It expressed the journey of a whole age of people... it hit the nail on the head and there was massive unity across the world... Marc was much more into that than the Stones were, he was more modern than the Stones. They played old R&B; Marc went out on a limb a bit.... There was something magic about him, like a pixie... Basicaly he just yelled out what he felt and was clever enough and really musical.

I wore the suit at parties, but all the jet bits would come off and then I grew out of it... I took the pony back when he died... it later fell on me and broke my ankle... I didn't see him towards the end. He was whirled away into the vortex of the rock star life and I was more in the country."

Barry "X"

How did you get into gambling, and, more specifically, blackjack?

Well probably, gambling-wise, it's been right from my parents, y'know, ever since I was small, dog tracks and that. I was managing betting shops at sixteen, so it's always been around. Always looking for some sort of easy way to make a few quid, always looking for an edge. I don't feel that I'm just sort of a blind gambler. Just 'cos I'm not doing any good at poker [Barry is also professional poker player] I won't go and play craps. So I won't knowingly play without some sort of opinion. And then I got involved with a very well known guy in the blackjack field called Don Fraser, who's sort of like a guru in this country. He set up a a a blackjack team to go to Malasia to play and I went to see him, and he said, "You've got a bit to learn," y'know, "learn this, learn that." and, anyway, he taught me quite a bit.

What did he teach you, how to count cards?

Yeah, I mean you can learn counting from a book, but then the reality of playing in a casino is — I mean, you can play on your kitchen table, and you can become very proficient, but there's a certain level you need to reach before you could ever go into a casino. But even once you reach that level some people can't hack it once they sit at the table. I went on a team with this guy — we went to Vegas for the first time in '83, a little six man team it was, and one of the guys, who was very, very capable whenever we did any testing or role plays and things, well, he just cracked up.

What, you mean at the actual table, inside a casino?

Yeah, he could not physically bring himself to put any big money because of the heat we got there.

"Heat" being the close attention given to you by the pit bosses?

Exactly. So what I'm saying is, it's very much a temperamental thing once you've got a certain skill level. Anyway, so I played blackjack solely from '83, right through to '87, four years of it, and, well, it's not just counting, I mean there's lots of things that lead on from counting that give you a much bigger advantage.

Such as?

Well, there's shuffle tracking, exploiting the weakness of the shuffle.

And what are you tracking? All the Aces? The paints [picture cards]?

Yeah, yeah, certain sections of cards or even individual cards…

Really!? Wow…

Yeah, but I won't go into that because…

What? It's a secret?

Well, no, it's… um… a bit technical.

Right. And what would you say is the difference between playing in Vegas and London?

They felt, in Vegas, at that time, there wasn't anything that they couldn't spot. When we got there, immediately we got heat, 'cos if you've got any kind of money… they're waiting for the bigger bets, so they think you're a counter straight away. Well when we started playing there, we weren't counting at all, we were just locating sections of cards, exploiting weak shuffles. So sometimes we would be betting when there were plus counts, minus counts, level counts, but every time we had a bet we were getting good cards. They brought in experts to watch the play and they said, "Oh they're not counting, let 'em play", and so we made quite a bit of money.

Confessions of a professional Blackjack player

How much?

About 300 thousand dollars in 6 months.

Was this by yourself or...

No, no it was a team, a three man team. We really had a thing going there, we won 30 or 40 thousand, probably, one night. I mean, the heat was amazing. We were fully comped, we had the whole of the top floor of the Dunes, at one stage, there was three of us plus a few girls, that sort of thing. They were trying to make it very comfortable so that we would lose what we were winning. It was me and, well, I'll call them Johnny and Frankie, and they [the Dunes] were paying our air fares – y'know, giving us good food, I mean the expenses were phenomenal, they were picking it all up, because they felt they were going to get the money.

And how did you do it, were you just three friends playing or...?

Well, what happened was Johnny was the "big player", supposedly someone in the music business, I was the so-called minder, and Frankie was like his "road manager". So he's off playing craps and coming back, and we were signalling Johnny when to bet. Johnny was doing the social bit, drinking Dom Perrignon at the table, I mean many nights getting really fuckin' drunk, y'know, we used to give him a terrible time sometimes 'cos he missed signals and different things y'know, but, uh, it was a really good act. I was standing behind him all the time and we had an audible signal that he would bet with, so he would be talking and that, not looking at the cards, and all of a sudden he'd get the signal and go from two hands of twenty-five dollars to two or three of three thousand dollars, which was the maximum there at the time, and they thought it was on a whim and a fancy.

So after a casino barred you, what were some of the disguises you wore?

I had a false moustache, I used to wear, like, the old style peak cap, y'know, real old English style. I got some stuff out of a charity shop like the wide check – I looked eighty years of age. I got some special glasses that were really, really thick – I mean even my kids never recognised me. Old shirt... really good disguise, I've sat next to people, y'know, who really know me well and they didn't have a clue.

So tell me more about your "act", I mean, you must have been tracking and counting, but not looking as though you were.

Yeah, it's easy to do when you're counting, but while you're shuffle tracking it's a bit more difficult 'cos you've got to keep your eye on the discard pile a lot more, and you've got to watch what's happening during the shuffle as well. Most pit bosses in Vegas are taught how to count. I can spot a player within a couple of minutes, you just have an instinct. I can tell somebody who's makin' out he doesn't know what he's doing, and somebody who really doesn't know what he's doing, so you have to give that impression that you're regular player, it's not always easy to do. More so in the States, you need a good act, 'cos they'll stop you very quickly and just say they don't want your action anymore.

Interview by Hugo Martin

MUSEUMS OF THE MUNDANE

Things I have bought in the charity shops of London: a copy of Kurt Vonnegut's Slaughterhouse Five containing an unused ticket for Led Zeppelin at Earl's Court in 1975; the first Mark Riley And The Creepers album; six hours of used blank tapes containing some compellingly dreadful bedroom demos followed by a fierce argument between two of those responsible.

All of these objects carry their own secret history. They're useless, as most things in museums are, yet they offer a tantalisingly brief glimpse into nameless lives and abandoned obsessions. In Crouch End I found a crate of scratched old dub albums – the launch pad for an obsession of my own – a pair of DMs and a small collection of *The Raven* – Anarchist Quaterly magazine. In Wood Green I found a book written by a friend's Father. In Brixton I bought what I took to be a uniquely patterned paisley shirt, only to discover that a close acquaintance had discarded it after a particularly heavy night on the sauce.

Charity shops then, are cultural deep freezers, the keepers of society's ephemera. Every object has it's own tale to tell, its own previous life. As such they occupy a unique place in the High Street. The musty smell of dog-eared paperbacks, the slightly uncomfortable sensation that someone may have died while wearing your coat, combine to produce an air of still life for sale.

This may be why charity shops have an inescapable air of melancholy. Like museums and libraries, they attract society's least loved: the old, the skint and the curious. We skulk about fingering the remnants of other people's lives, buoyed up by the same clandestine competitive spirit which moves middle aged women to queue up all night outside Cliff Richard concerts: irrational, inexplicable yet strangely irresistible.

As consumers we differ from other shoppers in that we're not looking for something, we're looking for anything. We live for the victorious rush which accompanies a genuine find, buzzed up by the knowledge that ten minutes later it might have disappeared out of our lives forever. In the charity shop, as indeed in life, chance is everything.

I have travelled all over the capital in search of little treasures. Time was when you could judge a neighbourhood by the local pub. But now that most pubs have, ironically, remodelled themselves in the style of Victorian junkyards (walls adorned with unidentified farming implements, lonely old boots, keys, bullets and washers mounted in cases) it's only through an area's charity shops that a stranger can hope to fathom the minds of those who live there.

I prefer the genteel suburbs of north London – Muswell Hill, Belsize Park, Highgate – where ladies of a certain age grapple awkwardly with the mechanics of the till. The most pertinent lesson to learn from these establishments is that nothing is for life. Stroking a stained leather jacket, I imagine first-time home buyers offloading the trappings of their youth: one-time dope-smoking seditionaries sifting through the contents of their spare rooms and attics, shaking their heads in wonderment that the person who bought all those Theatre of Hate albums ever existed. Their consignment to the charity shop marks the death of their former selves. Simultaneously intimate and anonymous, charity shops are full of stranger's memories.

For my own part, I cannot bear to part with anything, new or otherwise. My purchases are for life. For the time being.

Jon Fortgang

A FIVER FOR JAKE... by Gavin Clarke

We accompanied 7-year-old Jake Cadbury on a trip round the charity shops of Penzance, Cornwall. Visiting a couple of the best looking shops around and armed with a fiver, here's what he came up with:

1) Small plastic electric guitar offering battery-operated simulations of heavy metal lead breaks. Cost 50p. Jake says: "I chose this 'cos it looks like very fun and makes a loud noise".

2) Ornamental barometer with crystals in glass vial that forecast the weather. Picture of Truro Cathedral mounted on wooden base. Cost £1 Jake says: "This can tell me the weather so I know if I can go out."

3) Plastic monkey on a real shell. Cost 45p. jake says: "I just think it looks nice, and it was cheap. I expected it to be more like £1."

4) Moonwashed denim jacket with stripey lining, circa early 80s. Cost: £1.95. Jake says: "I got this cos it looks modern, and I can go motorcycling in it. It fits, too."

5) Small, solid brass statue of 'Kingry VIII', as Jake calls him. Cost 40p. He says: "It looks nice. I like kings. It was cheap."

Iggy Pop

Iggy Pop is God – what else can I say? I ran into him in the bowels of the Continental. It was pitch black in there but my senses told me I was in a divine presence. I was afraid to approach Iggy because he is someone who is truly a superstar and is bigger than life. I am glad I did not know at the time that Iggy can be really rude to slavering persons who approach him. I am happy to say this wasn't the case with me.

Dee Dee Ramone

I ran into Dee Dee Ramone outside tower records. Dee Dee Ramone is one of the nicest guys I've ever met. He told me he and his wife had just moved into a new apartment. We chit chatted about nothing much. Dee Dee looks healthy, wealthy and wise. Dee Dee is the Ramones.

Tav Falco

I ran into Tav at a club when he was performing in town, he was minus the panther burns. Tav is really into his Tango Dancing which he does with his lovely girlfriend Claudia. Tav has a reputation of being an asshole but we hung out a lot, and he is definitely stuck on himself but no asshole. I lent Tav a Tommy Nutter suit and he looked magnificent in it.

Kelley
Ryan

Celebrity Stalker

Jayne County

Formerly Wayne County of Wayne County and the Electric Chairs. Famous for bashing in Handsome Dick Manitoba's head with a mike stand because Handsome Dick kept screaming 'Faggot' from the edge of the stage and baiting Jayne. They had to do a benefit for Handsome Dick while he was in hospital. Wayne/Jayne is also famous for the songs 'Max's Kansas City' which is an anthem to the Max's scene. Other Jayne County songs include 'If You Don't Wanna Fuck Me Baby, Then Fuck Off' and 'I'm Stuck on You', not to mention 'You Make Me Cream in My Jeans'. Jayne uses Maybelline and we had a discussion about this in the lady's room at a club. Jayne is more woman than I could ever be.

Richard Hell

Richard Hell is one of my idols. I accosted Richard at his very own art opening somewhere in the bowels of the meat packing district. Richard Hell is the voice of the Blank Generation. Read his new novel, whatever it's called.

Joey Ramone

Joey Ramone is a very tall shy quiet person who said absolutely nothing but agreed to let me have a picture with him. Nuff said.

CLIVE SINCLAIR

Philosophy

I try to come up with a product that people hadn't thought they needed, that can change their lives and make them more cheerful.

First calculator

I invented the pocket calculator in the early 70s. 1972. I went to Smiths and they turned it down! With radical products, retailers are incredibly conservative. I launch products by mail order. Advertising in mags saved my bacon.

First home computers

The ZX 80, the first one, was technically difficult. Computers were £1000, and by design, I got the price under £100. It was a hobbyist and technophile market but it took off like a rocket, became best-selling. It had a 2K memory and the ZX81 was 4K [a computer now is 65,000K or so] Someone wrote a chess program on that. People learned to control computers but there's an appallingly inefficient use of memory. I'm keen to design one again.

The Sinclair C5

The C5 got very bad press. We could've introduced it more gently. People resist change. This is natural because for most animals a change is for the worse. When the first bicycles took to the road people threw stones at them. It's interesting that the new A–class Mercedes Benz was introduced gently. There's a chap advertising C5s now for £2,000.

People said they were dangerous, they felt insecure because they were low down. It would be different on cycle tracks but in London it's not the answer. The ultra lightweight bike might make a difference in this way.

Why not billionaire?

My role is initiating something, after a while they become standardised commodities. I'm not interested in that, I'm only interested in new ideas and technology. The home computer thing was significant and that's enough.

Bicycles

The Zeeta 2 converts bicycles to practical electric power. It stems from problems with energy. Electric cars are being done so I don't bother with them.

Bicycles haven't got any lighter for 100 years. I'd like to do a dramatically lighter and more compact bicycle that you can take on and off the tube – something you can carry around like an umbrella and take in to work – you've got to lock normal bikes. I spent time and money on the X bike, which was 20lb but I didn't feel that it did the job. We simply need a better folding cycle, so I'm working on Son of X which has a much more radical drive system and I want to get it to 8lb. I played with taking up recumbents and made a chassis to test it. It wasn't as stable and because you were low you couldn't see over cars. They're wonderful but they don't go as well up hills and I can't work out why. The conventional position is best. Son of X will be a lot more efficient and less wind resistant. I'm very optimistic.

POPPY

She's FIT

found

My collection of found writing started with a pair of saucy letters from a prisoner to his girlfriend that fluttered into my path as I walked to work one sunny morning. I wondered how such intimate belongings could have got there, I imagined the recipient throwing the letters contemptuously from her car window as she sped away from him forever, or maybe they just fell from her pocket while she was looking the other way, trying to cross the road. Since then my collection has grown, it is now contained in a large box file, and here I must give thanks and love to Kay Hyatt, Simon Murphy, Jeremy and Jane Cooper and Hilary Russian for passing on to me things they've acquired. I collect pretty much any found writing as long as it has a kind of home-made feel to it: shoping lists, torn cards, misdirected mail, letters, odd little notes, homework. I peel rain-soaked paper from the pavement and take it home to dry on the windowsi!l, torn or whole, it doesn't matter to me.

The thing I love best is sneaking a peek at somebody's private life, where big themes of love, hate and hope are often rendered banal and clichéd, which I find funny, or at other times the writing is so poignant I think I'll die. I am touched by the awkward voices of people not used to expressing themselves in writing, indeed when most of the writing in my life is proffessionalised through the mangle of copy and subediting, typesetting, then presented neatly or dynamically, it almost feels like a release to find words that are unashamadly amateurish, though real to the writer. You can't go looking for writing like this, it's a random pleasure that just falls into your life like a gift from heaven.

These pieces are largely anonymous, but if I've included something that belongs to you and you want it back, please write.

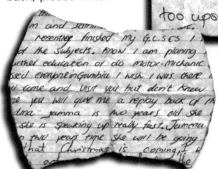

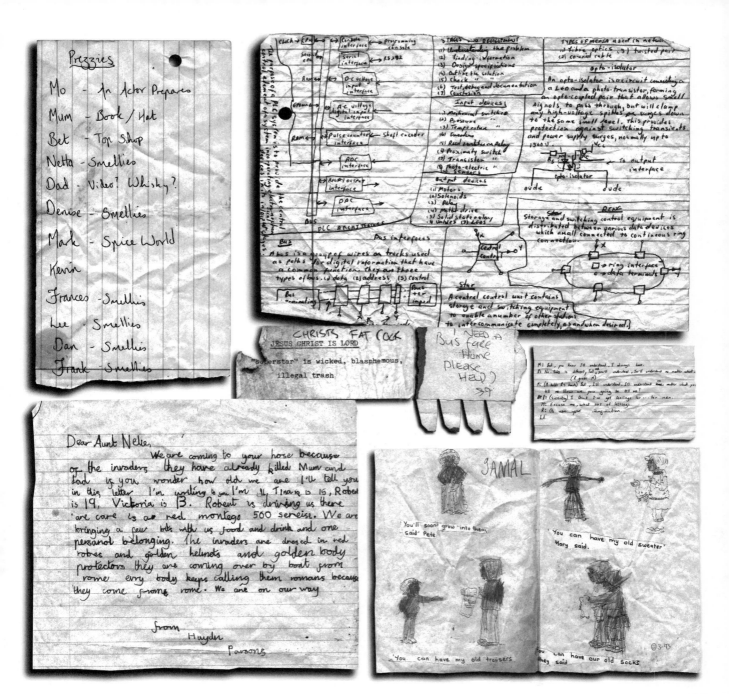

GENE SIMMONS

Is Kiss is an important band?

Let's be honest. there's nothing that we do that's original. It's really devoid of content, but so are most of the things that I love. I went to see *Independence Day* and I was so blown away by it.

Like all things American, you can't wait to revel in the size of it all. Kiss are the biggest band in the world and that means we're the best. Anybody who tells you they want to create something meaningful is lying, it's just their route to being BIG. Kiss realize that and just go for it. We invented the meaning of big American music, stadium rock, big stage show. It's what everyone wants. Things that mean something? I DON'T CARE. "Oh but it's about human nature." I DON'T CARE. I'm alive, I want to enjoy life, I want to be amazed, take me on a ride, take me to Disneyland, take me to Las Vegas, I want to live, turn me upside down. TAKE ME!

Why is it that you're still popular?

Because we're not fashionable.

Is that a good or a bad thing?

I was never a fan of fashion. I always found the idea of of it so bizarre. Fashion is a dog chasing it's tail and going nowhere fast. Anyone who's dedicated to fashion I find a little bit pathetic because they want to be accepted. It's a waste of energy, mindless lemmings doing it because there's safety in numbers.

What about clothes fashion?

Women wearing clothes designed by men who aren't clear of their sexual inclinations, in Paris – or something like that.

Does not craving critical recognition help keep the Kiss torch aflame?

I hope we never get credibility with the media, because it comes with a very heavy price. It comes with the idea that what I have to say above and beyond music is important, and that's the biggest load of crap I've ever heard. Jo Rockstar who six months ago couldn't wipe his ass, gets a platinum record and suddenly we give him access to talk about rainforests. We're guilty of letting the clowns have credibility. Just because we can write a song doesn't mean we know about the nature of existence. Each one of us gets our own soap box, but it doesn't mean we're smarter, if fact often we're dumber – we're a pretty dumb bunch. The public is fickle – they have the right to say, "Right I've had enough of you lot, bye bye."

You must work pretty hard.

We're getting away with murder. What I do is loafing. It means nothing. I get paid hideous amounts of money, women want to have my children, just because of my job. Heaven knows if I was out there digging a ditch they wouldn't look twice. I'm hideously ugly. Well, I said that for effect. The building we're sitting in now, which stands on top of a street – somebody had to dig the ditches, make the foundation and build it. Every day they'd get up, work from dawn till dusk at something they didn't want to do. Imagine doing that every day and at the end of the day you go home, your back aching and the next day you do the same thing. That's work. For the rest of your life. Without anybody saying "Wow that's great. Look at that brick you just laid." No public applause, no appreciation, nothing. Yet they do a great job. Poor people don't have as many psychological problems because they don't endlessy question their lives. They're just trying to get on. If you're poor you're worried about everything. when you're rich, you worry about less important things and start creating problems. This building will stand the test of time. That's work. That's you too. We get away with murder. Every day something new happens.

Today they showed me these Kiss dolls that are coming out. They're fabulous. A million of them are being made. Here's a Kiss comic book. Two more big orders for my Kiss bass guitar that I manufactured. *Kiss Rocks the World* magazine we put out ourselves and I get to put in what I want. Why would I consider that work? I strike it lucky every day of my life. "I just want just enough to get by" is a lie. I don't just want to get by, nor does anybody. I want it all. I'm just like everybody else – I always want more. It's a matter of being in the right place at the right time. The idea really is that this is not work, and the least I can do is, if you love what you do, is I can't wait to get up in the morning.

You seem quite down to earth.

I know that what I eat may not be anybody else's cup of tea. Somebody likes to eat octopus tentacles with their suction cups but not me. It's all personal choice. My mother loves me whether I'm a rock star or not.

Do you enjoy a rock'n'roll lifestyle?

I've never once been high in my life on drugs and that's the truth, and I've never been drunk. But I do like the girls. It's not a vice. Everyone's got their thing and they should do it as often as they can. It's a personal kind of happiness. I want to fuck as many women as I can, all the women in the world. What are you doing later?

Operation Clothes Care

Ironing

The correct – and quick – way to iron a blouse or shirt is to do it in this order. With the garment turned inside out, first iron the sleeves and then the cuffs. Next do the shoulders followed by the back; then the two fronts. Last of all iron the collar.

If you don't have a sleeve board, improvise by folding a towel in half lengthways and rolling it up tightly. You may be a bit clumsy at first but you will soon become adept at managing it.

I know that many materials nowadays are supposed not to require ironing, but the truth is that they all look better for it.

While we are on the subject of ironing, why are hair ribbons so neglected, I wonder?

Brushes

Don't overlook the clothes-brush, will you? Pocket-sized brushes are obtainable cheaply, and there is just no excuse for stray hairs and old bits of fluff. In fact, a girl's best friends are her brushes; clothes brush, hair brush and shoe brush. Use them all vigorously and with unfailing regularity and you cannot fail to look smarter. You will *feel* spick and span.

Pleats

If you are lucky enough to possess a permanently pleated skirt in nylon or Terylene, ironing will be unnecessary, but the secret of crisp pleats rests in the way the skirt is dried. After washing according to the manufacturers' directions, rinse at least twice, and then carry the skirt out to the clothes line in a blowl of water. Peg it up by the waistband using three pegs and then leave it to stream. The weight of the water will remove all creases and pull the pleats into position so that they dry properly knife-edged once more.

Stain Removing

Make a pad of clean material and place it underneath the mark, soak a piece of cotton wool in cleaning fluid and press down hard on the stain. Repeat several times using clean cotton wool and continually turning the pad so that you are always pressing on to a clean surface.

Ball-point ink can be removed by the same method – substituting methylated spirits for the cleaning fluid. These marks must be dealt with promptly, however, for if they are left to dry for a few days they will become quite immovable.

Nico's Super

Photographs: Faye Norman

No, this is not the cloakroom, but you can swap your coat for my boots.

The club is busy tonight. People are dancing and drinking and chatting. Two girls in the toilets are frowning at their reflections and pulling at their clothes, their cigarettes burning into the washstands, their drinks diluting beside them. "I'm sick of this dress!" says one, rubbing on lipstick and mussing up her hair. "I always wear it out" "I know what you mean," says her friend in the spangly top. "Not your dress – it's lovely – but look at me! When I was getting ready I thought I looked great but now I hate it! "

If only they knew that Nico's Super Swops was in town again! Some early clubbers have already discovered the brightly-lit obstacle on their dance floor. It is loud and busy, and at the swap stall the pointing, picking and giggling has started. A girl disappears into the little changing room while her friends go through the goods on the clothes rail. Nico, the goggle-wearing stall minder, is busy negotiating with 2 new customers. At the top of her voice, making big gestures to illustrate her point, she is trying to do business: "Like your top. Wanna swap for anything? I think you'd fit that dress… Sure, you can try it on, here's the changing room and there's the mirror… Looks great on you, want to make a deal?… Well, your sock is not enough I'm afraid, and I don't take any money either… Know what? You give your trousers to your friend, I'll have her skirt and you'll have my dress. Have a great time, girls!"

As the two happy customers make their way to the bar, Nico smiles to herself. "Buying is so boring," she thinks, putting a label (swap 106) inside the newly obtained skirt and hurriedly making an item description in her notebook (thus trying to keep track of the history of her shop). From the very first swap deal (a boy giving his eyebrow piercing for a cowboy hat), to the next one (a few American kids have already put their eyes on number 106, a chance to gain something foreign), she is always surprised how easily people embrace the spirit of the cashless shop. It was freezing cold one night, and a girl swapped her lacy tights for a plastic mac; another time a guy swapped his combat trousers and body warmer for a pair of pyjamas. She had to give him a carrier bag for his mobile phone!

Swops

But it's not only spontaneous greed on seeing beautiful clothes that make the shop successful. What started off as an exploration of barter, value and personal attachment sometimes becomes a little haven of generosity. Once, at the end of a long night of swapping, a customer returned to the shop, not to undo a deal made earlier, but to give Nico his necklace: "All my friends say I look great in this shirt, so this is for you." In moments like that, she wants to become a missionary, spreading the swapping spirit all over the money obsessed town of London!

Nico's Super Swops has been travelling from club to club for a year now. And (ha!), sometimes it seems that it's spirit and fame have exceeded it's little world. She remembers seeing an old customer at a party on her night off, giving the flowery shirt that she'd swapped with him weeks before (the label with the swap number still inside it) to a stage dancer. And the girl collecting glasses in a packed bar, pinching her, going "remember?" while pointing at her trousers. Or the boy in the bus (was it the one that swapped his ear protectors?) making the 'wanna swap?' gesture to her before getting off.

What more reason does she need to keep setting up her stall? She can promote the fun of cashlessness and do herself a favour at the same time, because in her fastly changing swap collection, there's always a brand new outfit waiting for her. She'll never have to hate what she's wearing out. Ever again.

Nico Van Harskamp
thanks to Helga and Amp

To increase the variety and the fun, Nico's has started a middle man service. Everyone bored by their wardrobes can ask Super Swops to swap max 10 items for them – given they make a pretty collection. A mini banner will be provided. The swap girl can't guarantee business (last time, there was a rush for 'Helga's', whereas 'Debra's' was deserted – it must have been the kind of club, Deb!), but she'll do her best to make deals that match the owner's taste. Helga, for example, was pleasantly surprised, but then, she had been hassling people on the dance floor all night. For info contact Nico.

Nico's Super Swops will come to your party! for fifty pounds and/ or travel expenses, contact Nico on nicolinev@hotmail.com for negotiations and bookings

What are you *collecting* at the moment *Mark*?

You mean other than Gonks, Plastic Moustaches, Small Plastic Babies, Kinder Egg Toys, Noggins/ Vikings and Figures that Piddle?

Well I'd have to say the 50s/60s Jokey novelty drink coasters, ashtrays and similar items that I've quietly accumulated over the last year, about 30 pieces now – a full-blown collection, I've even got doubles!

The first things I came across were the wooden coasters with bar-room humour type jokes and wisecracks printed on them, with simple cartoon graphics and hand-lettered slogans, featuring a recognisable cast of Happy Drunks, top-hatted Toffs, good-time Gals and icepack-on-head Hangover victims.

We're talking lowbrow unapologetic Drinkin' fun here, blue–collar Bourbon Binges not Cocktail Cool.

I like the cheapness of them, then as now, printed in red and black on wood–the plastic of it's day, they're mass produced and authorless with generic gags– the same slogan can turn up with slight variations and different illustrations.

In addition to coasters which originally came in sets of six, there's ashtrays, a couple of Wall Plaques/ Signs and some Spanking Sticks aka 'Fanny Paddles' aka 'Wife Beaters' all with similar gags and graphics.

CONSUMER INFORMATION

Where? Boot Sales/Junk shops/Camden Market
How Much? Mostly 10p-£1 and up to a massive £4 for the 'You're in the Dog House' sign with rotating disc giving six explainations-whic is also my current favourite.

Everything I like is either Illegal, Immoral or fattening

GRIP HERE FIRMLY IN CASE OF FRUSTRATION

For the Cute Little Deer WITH THE Bear BEHIND

BOARD OF EDUCATION ** APPLIED PSYCHOLOGY

"ENJOY YOURSELF" IT'S LATER THAN YOU THINK!!!

A CAMEL CAN GO WITHOUT a DRINK for 8 days BUT WHO WANTS TO BE a Camel?

IRIS

THE
VIRUS

The Wreckless

It's all about the rights of the individual – nothing to do with anything old, retro cheap, dusty or cobwebbed. And there's nothing wrong with wanking either – even doctors do it. I say do what you like but don't be lonely. I lived in rural France for nine years. Everything there is old, dusty and cobwebbed, retro

hasn't yet been invented and most of it's cheap – including life itself.

I must have spent months of my life looking at fields through cracked windscreens on the way to and from the nearest town with any shops, circumnavigating near-death experiences on every other bend courtesy of some macho latino retard in a Renault Five with a second hand spoiler. The French countryside is cluttered with macho latino retards, and there isn't much for them to do except court near death experiences in cheapo cars with budget customisations. That and wanking of course.

Nowadays (as opposed to the Good Old Days when France was limbering up to become retro capital of the world), the sides of barns and derelict houses which used to display those archetypal French "Dubonnet" murals are pasted over with CUM 3615 advertising – wall sized visions of loveliness – a temptress in the buff with the word CUM obscuring the *ooh la la* bits. And frustrated French Romeo's wank themselves into bankruptcy via the internet.

Except on Saturday nights. Saturday nights is disco night and Mrs

Fist stays home to wank another week away while the latino macho retard recovers in intensive care from totalling the Renault. On Sunday mornings you see them on their roofs in the middle of fields, hanging off trees, lounging in ditches…

Of course that's for the older youngsters – you've got to be over eighteen to get into the foam party at the defunct chateau turned disco. The younger ones dream of turning fifteen so they can buy a clapped-out moped and ride on over to the next village to sit in a different bus shelter for an evening. The moped is a popular form of transport for anybody under disco age, old men in rubberised macs and peaked helmets, and middle-aged women who like to put their shopping in the panniers and ride them wearing quilted anoraks. Nutters ride mopeds too. They loom out of the fog in a whirring and buzzing cloud of two stroke, and tap on your window at three o'clock in the morning when you're sleeping in a lay-by, and ask for directions to Rouen.

They wear old brown corduroy that looks like dried-up mud, and when they pass on the relatives come from Paris or somewhere and palm it

Over-view

all off on the local "Ding Fring" charity shop where it hangs around looking like a patchwork of ploughed fields. next to the slightly more groovy corduroy clothes belonging to deceased Saturday Nite wankers.

Not that France can claim a monopoly on nutters. Wankers possibly, but not nutters. You get them everywhere – especially the clothing oriented ones, like the policewoman in the home made uniform and toy gun ensemble who used to direct the traffic on Broadway, or Joe Gunwire née Injun Joe Seawheel who lived on the corporation tip in Hull and made public appearances on a bicycle wearing boxing gloves and decoy duck headgear.

But France is rural and the rural nutter is special – there's much more raw material – shops that sell hunting gear, bricolage shops that make the B&Q look like Mothercare – that sort of thing. And much more space in which to be special. ("Special" is a word that the French use quite a lot in conjunction with nutters – I heard it used in conjunction with me a couple of times.) It's like Blue Peter really – you'll need lots of rolls of different coloured electricians tape, empty soup

tins and some old dexion to make a model of the Eiffel Tower for the garden. Then you cover the front of the house with oyster shells and – voilà.

Then you stroll round the village in a cowboy outfit and turban – at least our nutter did, except in winter when he wore his mothers old quilted anorak. He rode a moped too. Once during a blizzard we saw him piss on the engine in an attempt to warm it up sufficiently to start the thing.

Myself I never did any of these things, although my Farfisa organ is plastered with red, white and green electricians tape (it is an Italian organ) to hold the extraneous cables from my many customisations in place. I always wanted to cover the outside of the house with oyster shells and hub-caps but as it was rented it didn't seem worthwhile. I just lived in a shack and made pop records.

Eric Goulden

Budget Suave

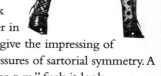

Odd Socks

Where once wearing odd socks designated a lack of clean laundry and/or reckless flouting of dress etiquette, it can now be seen as a louche signifier of decadent indifference. For instance, designer sock cast-offs like Paul Smith (picked up by this writer in a charity shop for a quid – an unmatching pair) give the impressing of being loaded enough not to worry about the pressures of sartorial symmetry. A sort of "fell out of bed and into a pink gin at three p.m." fuck it look.

No Try, Only Do

As Roy Castle always wailed: "Dedication's what you need…" and that's the thing you see. Look sharp requires discipline, especially on low income but you have to decide if you've got the strength to follow it through. There can be no room for half-heartedness, fakers of tourists. Get out on the street, dolled up and rise above. Out with the crap and in with the flash! **Andrew Copeman**

Betamax

The Betamax video cassette recorder (VCR) was the first real victim of a directly contested technology format war. Those that purchased them back in the early 80s are now seen as foolish and are the butt of many jokes. "Yeah, my parents bought a Betamax... how could they have been SOOOO stupid?"

The Betamax was Sony's foray into the home video market and had to compete with JVC's VHS format. VHS initially allowed for twice the one hour recording time of the Betamax, and it was this which meant that Sony was losing the war in the US by the time that home video arrived in the UK.

Initially many video rental shops were split, literally down the middle, offering both Beta and VHS. Others chose to specialise in one format or the other. But as Sony lost market share the supply of rental tapes dwindled too. Specialist Beta rental shops either closed down or started to stock VHS. The lack of choice for the Beta customer lead many to ditch their machine in favour of the VHS, especially in the flexible rental market.

In 1988 Sony held up their hands and produced their first VHS machine. Betamax was dead. Official.

My own memories of Betamax are from around 1983 when the possession of a VCR was becoming fairly common. And as far as I can remember, disillusionment with the format was already beginning to appear.

I was dating a girl whose parent had decided on, in her words: "a crappy Betamax," whilst her friend across the street had a VHS and parents with a blossoming porn collection. Needless to say this is where we spent the afternoons of our summer holidays, drinking really bad coffee, smoking Rothmans and watching *Debbie Does Dallas* and *I Spit on Your Grave*. Ahh, the sweet days before anyone cared if kids took out slasher movies and sex films.

Beta users always claimed, and still do, that theirs was the superior format. This may be borne out by the fact that it is still used, albeit in a different form, in the Television industry today.

You can still pick up Betamax VCRs in junk shops and boot sales, and despite rumour to the contrary you can still buy blank Beta tapes (try John Lewis or search on-line). You will be taking a gamble if you don't see the machine up and running, but it could be worth it if you find a stack of wonderful straight-to-video Beta format films for next to nothing.

Iain Aitch

Sophie

The Bower Bird

I grew up in Northern Ireland where the decorating ethic, in all its fine completeness, was Kitchens is buff and Landings is brown and where the concept of collecting meant the saving of small pieces of string and scraps of brown paper in dressers generally painted over with orange and red circles and where beauty was regarded as an Occasion of Sin

Perhaps as a consequence of this I have all my adult life contrived to live in houses which I think are beautiful and which are crammed with examples of everything that money, oh alright then, not quite money, everything that I can buy or better still find.

One of my most treasured possessions is a blue and white patterned Irish jug its chinosierie design ancient and faded, with a crude tin handle attached – a wonderful example of the art of the Irish tinker, who for centuries travelled around the country mending pots and pans and delft. I'd got out of the car to look at a ruined gate lodge on a remote road in Monaghan when I saw the glimmer of something in a ditch and there my treasure was, lying in the mud intact. Every day it affords me pleasure to look at it filled with a bunch of flowers, not only because it is such a

pretty object, but because through it I reach back into the vanished Ireland of my childhood and into the lost everyday craft of attaching tin to china; not that it would be far more expensive to mend a jug than to buy a new one. Tinkering is a specialist art.

Equally the terracotta pots that I buy on my travels are more often than not riveted together with neat iron stitches and somehow look the better for this evidence of frugality and care and good husbandry. Nearly all the things I collected have got some connection with the everyday arts and bear the marks of the people who have used them and loved them for centuries. The words 'pristine condition' have no attraction for me. I like seeing that the things I new own while I'm around had a previous life and will retain something of my energetic love when it is passed on.

I move through a wreck of possessions, professing (since I can apply a high moral gloss on anything I choose to do) that his way I am both attaining a high plane of Zen-like transparency and alleviating infantile trauma. There is a wonderful book by Werner Muensterberger called *Collecting: An Unruly Passion* which explains to my heart's content something I have always known – that collecting is an instrument designed not only to allay a basic need brought on by early traumata but also as an escape hatch for feelings of danger and the re-experience of loss.

There's a line in Shakespeare – (there always is) which struck me with peculiar force when I read them in the Merchant of Venice, that passionate play about the weights and measures of the heart. "The world is still deceived by ornament" Bassanio sighs, and goes on, "thus ornament is but the guiled shore to a most dangerous sea." Indeed, and I hoisted my sail and sat out on that sea years and years ago and have now lost sight of the shore.

For as long as I remember, ornament has meant credibility to me, extras which added authenticity to my life whether it was filling the tree

house under the purple rhododendron with broken shards of china or getting myself up with kohl and jangling metal belts and gold lame to try to look like Hollywood's idea of Cleopatra when I first came to London and always, always collecting, so that as the years roll by, my houses became ever more filled with objects, layer upon layer, so that the rooms seemed encrusted, and even the attics and lofts are barnacled with wrack from the wash below.

In trying to analyse the disease, I came upon the idea that it was as though I were trying to compose and construct the semblance of a heritage, the aggregations that undisturbed or unvexed families had passed down through generations, and which Irish families had been denied by their history, but it is in Muensterberger's book that I've found the best explanation: basically things provide magic protection and shield the collector from new frustrations and anxieties:

"Provoked by early, possibly unfavourable conditions or the lack of affection of the part of not-good-enough mothering, the child's attempt toward self-preservation quickly turns to some substitute to cling to. Thus, he or she has a need to compensatory object of one or the other kind. This can also be interpreted as a self-healing attempt. In later life, this attitude leads to a biased weighting for more money or more possessions."

Of course it must also be said that I like the look of my Staffordshire dogs grinning from behind their woolly coats and my mad lambs with their silly faces not unlike the Duchess of York's perched on their bocage or curled up at the feet of goofy lions. I like the look of everything I've acquired over the years including pictures, sculptures, urns, games trunks, painting, prints, anonymous ceramics of dogs, lambs, lions and mournful women; ducks, sheep, fish and hens in every manifestation including living ones, flowers, fabrics from every corner of the globe, some held together by fragile seventeenth century silken threads, glass of every kind, Roman, Waterford, Lalique, decanters and jelly moulds and doorstops, runners and candlesticks and funnels; globes, books, baubles, indoor bowls, shells, croquet balls, old wood bowls, Berlin Work, stump work, motto ware, spongeware, needle-point,

Aubusson, tapestries, mugs and loving cups engraved with initials (not my own), porcelain, delft, oak, walnut, water-colours, rosewood, mahogany, boxes, silver, polescreens, lacquer ware, chinosierie, the gatherings of a gambler or certainly an addict gambling on acquisition rather than loss or drugs.

Once, years ago, when waiting for my daughter Rose, who was at King's College Cambridge, to join me after a lecture, I followed signs to the mysteriously named Kettle's Yard, and discovered one man's resolution to the dilemma of possessions. In those simple unsoliciting arrangements he showed there was dignity to possessing, that what mattered was the inner worth of the outward show. It was my first lesson in allowing myself to admit that collecting was not just an arbitrary disconnected series of events – which is the classic thing that addicts persuade themselves to believe. In their minds each event is isolated, unique, not to be repeated. When in fact, it is all along linked chain that holds your life together and the pure and salient fact about this passion (or infection) is that saturation point is never reached.

Polly Devlin

Big Foot

Do you remember that song "Your Feets Too Big…" by Fats Waller? Well I feel a bit like that every time I see a divine strappy, spangly shoe that simply does not fit. In fact I'm the ugly sister of the market/charity shoe rail. The glass slipper never fits.

When I was growing up, shoes held a fascination for me far beyond their ordinary usage as foot coverings. I vaguely remember a poem which told of a child's yearning for "buckled shoes, bow shoes, pretty pointy toe shoes, black shoes, wipe them on the mat shoes, that's the sort they'll buy." And it was.

The source of my fascination lay in the initials I heard people use about the wonderful Terry de Havaland glittery mules and Dior strappy shoes that my Mum collected. Initials like IWT shoes – which I later discovered meant International White Trash shoes, and FM shoes – work it out.

Looking at her shoe collection, which seemed an emporium of the most glamorous shoes in the world (although looking back of course it wasn't), was when I really fell in love with the enchanted landscape of shoes; I couldn't wait for the day when I would grow up and have access to this world, when I would be able to teeter around in 5 inch stillettos myself – when I would be able to inherit her collection. Alas I didn't reckon on growing up to nearly 6ft with feet to match.

So really nothing has changed, now I admire and long for the shoes my friends find in the market for £10, but they just simply do not fit me. Ever. It's not that I have extravagantly large feet (7 and a half) but the average female foot is 5-6 and in earlier generations were ever smaller, so the odds of finding a pretty old size 7 1/2 is rare. Presumably if 20 years ago you tracked down a great pair of 7 1/2, you wore them until they fell apart.

The one pair of shoes I keep hoping I might find in a thrift shop is a pair by Roger Viver. He made exquisite shoes, and they have become collectors items. But the odds are against it, for who would let these treasures out of their grasp? So now when I look for those great antique shoes of the past, I try not to mind that they will never fit. Cinderella can keep her glass slippers.

Bay Garnet

I Was a Teenage GOTH

Standing outside Camden Town tube station, August 1987: black canvas, spray-on jeans; six buckle winkle-pickers; artfully frayed white blouse worn over Sister Of Mercy T-shirt; cascading black hair crimped to a crispy wisp; cadaverous cheeks and pierced cartilage; Bukowski novel tucked into pocket of swishing leather coat; and next to him is me: hair so curly that no known gel, spray, clue or combination thereof can persuade it to stand up and spike; freshly laundered Siouxsie And The Banshees T-shirt (mum: "*A Kiss in the Dreamhouse* – that sounds nice, dear"); newly pierced ear – still a little painful; and virginal Doc Martens – very painful indeed.

I am down from the suburbs to indulge the shadowy fantasies my friends and I have summoned up from a motley collection of obscure LPs and the pages of *Sounds*. We have come to sample the dark stuff, and possibly buy Mission T-shirts. We are teenage goths, and we smell of patchouli and Daz.

I can no longer remember where or when the Goth aesthetic entered my life, only the force with which it did so. In many way ways it represented the perfect youth cult; ridiculous, vain, pretentious and partisan in the extreme. The music upon which it hung itself has not, with a few notable exceptions (Killing Joke, Nick Cave) stood the test of time; all those minor chords, eerie wind noises and grand sentiments seem, from the downsized nineties, absurdly self-inflated.

And yet in style and in attitude, Goth represented the purest distillation of seedy, sleazy, nasty rock n roll. It was self-obsessed, insular, largely humourless and bound by strict behavioural and dress codes: an entirely appropriate response to life in Thatcher's Britain.

Nick Cave and Siouxsie Sioux can probably claim to have spawned the Goth style, which broadly speaking married junkie chic with big hair. It's heritage took in the Romantic poets (enigmatic, frequently wasted, nice line in frilly shirts), vampirism as described by Werner Herzog in Nosferatu, and, in a way I never really understood, the architecture of Berlin. But most of all, Goth was spawned in the stalls of Camden Market. There you could, and indeed still can, find the chunky silver jewellery, the fetishistic leather, the faschistic (pre-crusty) army surplus gear. All available in black, or, for the more adventurous, new-bruise purple.

Illustrations: Laura Findley

Never mind that goths were almost exclusively middle class and lived with their parents in Amersham, or Surbiton, or Woking. At the weekend, skulking round Camden chewing cheap sulphate, or Snakebitten in the bowels of the World's End pub, they represented, as all good youth cults should, and aggressively elite club – somewhere where you could be simultaneously apart and a part.

And yet I never really felt I'd got it right. Attempts to peroxide my hair and cultivate a small beard left me looking like a baby George Micheal. A shabby tuxedo jacket and vermilion waistcoat made me look like a waiter. But perhaps the worst crime against fashion committed in the name of Goth was my decision to wear a hat. Normally, no male under pensionable age should wear a hat unless it's a helmet, but under the influence of The Mission and Fields Of the Nephilim, I trawled the Portobello Road for a black, wide-brimmed thing. This, I felt, would mark my graduation from under-goth to master-goth. From beneath it's brim my flinty gaze would scour passers-by. There he goes, people would whisper. The man in the hat…

But instead, even my goth mates took the piss. Travelling on the bus, small children would try to knock it off. Babies dribbled over it. Shop assistants would ask me to take it off, and worst of all, I did. There is only one thing which looks more daft than a short-assed goth wearing a big hat, and that's a short-assed goth carrying a big hat. I lost it at a New Model Army gig in 1990.

By then though, dawn was beginning to break over the long, dark night of Goth, and it wasn't long before my friends and I purged our record collections, our wardrobes and our photo albums with Stalinist zeal. It's the perogative of every twentysomething to reinvent their past without reference to the facts, but sometimes, late at night, in moments of weakness, or when we spy a tell-tale piece of chunky Celtic jewellery, we exchange a sly smile of recognition and whisper the words: I was a teenage Goth.

Jon Fortgang

Budget Suave

Brogue Trooper

Polishing shoes seems the easiest thing in the world, whack on the Kiwi shine and rub furiously. However, do not be lulled into a false sense of security: buffing is an art-form, demanding Zen-like concentration and the correct equipment. Two brushes are needed, small and large, the former for applying the polish, the latter for buffing it off. The width and density of the bristles is crucial; too narrow and not enough polish will be applied, too big and you're in danger of clogging up the pores. Modern bristles tend to be made of plastic fibre and whilst they get the job done, they fail to compete with old fashioned horse-hair; the stiffness of these disperse the correct quantities of polish and, on the whole, last longer. When applying polish it is important to brush in a circular motion, never back and forth, as this damages the leather. As a stress relief exercise, shoe maintenance is one of the best; the perfect syntheses of contemplation and style.

Andrew Copeman

by stephen Dreehan, June 1999

dream thrift

whatever became of all those lovely cartoony Pop Art red-with-green-stalk/spout plastic tomato-shaped ketchup dispensers? Brightening up many a yesteryear greasy spoon/burger bar table, these prime candidates for immortalisation in the form of a Claes Oldenburg giant soft sculpture have seemingly disappeared from view, been superseded by relatively unexciting cylindrical saucy squeezies with which to blast cinema blood at one's chips, beans and vegesausages.

* Some history: mass-manufactured in the rock'n'roll 'fifties, the Morris Friedman-designed moulded polyethylene (soft flexible plastic) tom was the first squeeze-bottle food dispenser. 1947 had seen the appearance of a Stopette deodorant container, the first squeezable of all, after cosmetics chemist Jules Montenier had perfected the squeezy bottle, working alongside Plax Corporation engineers. Initially adding colour to domestic kitchens, the tom soon became a restaurant favourite. The original tom was more realistic, smaller than the one I half-remember. The mould developed, the tomato becoming squarer, more stylised.

Memories are vague, frosted glass-hazy: not having encountered one such novelty fruity condiment container for two decades or more (in order to be able to safely contradict that kid's-eye-view, where objects always seem bigger than actual size) has resulted in what's maybe a distortion, an exaggeratedly handsome version/vision of something which could well disappoint, fail to meet adult expectations, and leave me futilely craving a more impressive never-really-existed fairytale tom.

Fellow Cheap Date-r Alvin Smith reckons the hinged-lidded (pull off, pop back on) tom was quite sizeable, like a comic strip bomb — and describes it as having possessed a Beano-esque quality: expected to have been employed by assorted Bash Street-ers upon their mountainous celebratory final frame bangers'n'mash (and, little doubt, upon the fizzog of swotty star pupil Cuthbert (cringeworthy). the tom certainly lent itself to mischief, to minxing and menacing: I've heard tell of how one could unscrew the cap, very carefully up-end the dispenser, and equally deftly place it upon the table, its cap precisely positioned on the wrong end. An unsuspecting customer would pick up the "innocent" tom for a hearty squeeze, sending a deluge of red gloop every which way.

Does anyone recall how brown sauce was previously presented? Was it simply poured straight from its slap-the-base glass bottle? Perhaps the absurd notion of a companion brown tomato (or was there one? Alvin thinks so – can any Wimpy regulars confirm this?), coupled with the appealing idea of the tidy matching pair with which we're familiar today, led to the tom's withdrawal. Or maybe so many folk considered the tom beautiful – and fun – enough to sidle out with one hidden under their coat that it was decided to discontinue them...?

Late 'nineties Wimpy ketchup comes in individual sealed sachets of silver, white and red – but how much for reasons of neatness and hygiene, and how much an anti-hooliganism measure? Brighton's Wimpy manageress speaks of red being squirted up the walls...

Whilst I'm growing both accustomed to, and quite fond of those tall, dimpled squeezy cylinders some caffs offer, they lack the humour and verve of the beloved tom. Of all my thrifting desires, the ketchup squeezy is probably my greatest obsession (and incidentally, I'd much prefer a battered old ex-someplace specimen with some history than a gleaming, unused, blemish-free model). Realistically, I know I'll never charity-shop a copy of Richard Brautigan's ultra-scarce (£450+!) 1968 Please Plant This Book (seed packets with poems printed on); and I've grave doubts about my local Heart Foundation chucking the half Japanese triple L.P. boxed set (complete with all inserts) my way. But this hunk of cheap red and green plastic seems equally frustratingly elusive. I want one!!

* BIBLIOGRAPHY

Andrea di Noto : Art Plastic – Designed For Living (New York : Abbeville, 1984)

Jeffrey L. Meikle : American Plastic – A Cultural History (New Brunswick, NJ : Rutgers University Press, 1995)

Henry Goodrich's Jodhpurs

In 1979 I started riding lessons. Convinced this would be a passing fad, my mother refused to pay out for new riding clothes so my riding instructor gave me a pair of Harry Hall jodhpurs outgrown by both her sons. The name tag inside told me that one of them was called Henry Goodrich. I continued to be pony-mad, however, and by the mid-80s we had moved to the countryside, kept our own ponies and my jodhpurs had been handed down to my brother. My mother, tapping into the great rural middle-class tradition of thriftiness, started a second-hand riding clothes and saddlery agency.

When he outgrew them, they went into the sale and were bought for a small girl, and her younger sister, and then back to my mother again. Over the next few years, they went out as an "extra pair" for Pony Club camp, or just for mucking out, coming back at regular intervals with more darns on the knee and hoof-oil stains. My mother always took them back, re-selling them for a token 75p, but then someone must have decided they were no longer fit for trade-in.

But by this time I was at sixth form and had discovered the delights of vintage clothing. Scouring Sussex jumble sales for bargains, I kept an eye open for anything horsey to sell – and one afternoon, I found some familiar-looking jodhpurs. The mysterious name inked inside the waistband confirmed that I had found my first pair again. In a sorry state by now, I gave them to a hard-up friend for her daughter. I then went away to university and lost touch with them – and my jodhpurs.

After my second student year, I spent the summer working in a stable yard. Hearing that my mother dealt in second-hand riding clothes, a woman asked me to find jodhpurs for her son. She gave me his scruffy old pair to show me the size – and there they were again! No longer remotely fit for Pony Club, I have them to another friend's little boy for dressing up in. A boxing fan, he puts them on to be Chris Eubanks. Now that's what I call value for money.

Farah AlKalisi

ZOE DRESSED TO KILL

The *Binner* Manifesto for
INTIMATE LIVING

Do you want to know about the shop next to the Hebrew Book and Gift Centre which throws away good vegetables? I could add a bit of local colour if you like and tell you about the old guy with the big beard who works in the shop, who gives me carrier bags so that I can take more food from his bin.

Would you like to know what I find there, that in the last few months I've taken from him fresh parsley, parsnips, baby turnips, plums, carrots, three kiwi fruits, cucumbers and a big bag of mushrooms?

Unless you were round my house when I cooked it, it's no more interesting than my telling you what I bought in the shops.

Binning is more than just the acquisition of things for free, and more than just a series of hyperbargains. I find things I need for nothing and I get excited, yet isn't gloating over possession of something still the acknowledgement, bred in us by an age of capitalism and commodity fetishism, that we can't do without it,

that the product is all we need, that even if we, the Binners, are hoovering up the mass market's waste and surplus, we are in some way saying If we had the money we'd buy it?

By finding my food on the street I am finding my food on the the street and that is all. I'm just feeding myself. I try not to take more than I need. All being a binner is, in this sense, is like being a maggot, part of the food chain, depending on others' money, waste and fastidiousness.

But if you pick up something which is not only unwanted but also unnecessary you become almost like it. You are like it already, or you will be.

By literally taking from the small bins which are all part of the big bin in which you and all your possessions will be, one day, or picking up that which is accidentally lost, and not thinking about the publishing deal you could get as result of writing about it, not the money you could earn by selling it, not the germs you catch by touching it, not the curry you could cook from it, by considering and thus valuing that which has, according to the

rules, no 'value', you might be also picking up the thoughts and connections on the outside, the edges of your world.

You might, of course, be doing nothing of the sort: the aesthetics of waste and loss are, necessarily, harder to define that those of production, consumption and gain, although it's even harder for us not to impose an aesthetic system, or, in fact any system at all. Like Luke Rhinehart's celebrations of the random in *The Dice Man,* which descends quite smoothly into writing prayers to the die, classifying and theorising on 'dice therapy' and even setting up centres, just in writing this stuff for this book I am chasing the dream of indefinable, pure, independent thought – and losing it in the big swamp of education, media-literacy and pompous prose style.

Would you like to read the letters I picked up from a street in Kensal Green, from a man in Wormwood Scrubs to his wife? Would you like to pore over his misspelt declarations of love and regret, savour the prison paper (it's funny size and shape), wonder what he did to get put there?

I would. I did. I'm a middle class voyeur too. You know and I know the

BOOT SALE

thrill of such material, the sympathy mixed with relief that *that's not me*, the intertextuality of our response based on the newspapers we've read, the episodes of *The Bill* we've watched, and the buildings we've walked past. If you're reading this kind of book, you've maybe also read *Inventory*, with its 'found text', so you know this letter's not only a piece of social documentary but also 'art', also the ultimate alternative literature.

So you get this shopping list instead. It's a list of colours. Maybe it'll make us think about the colours we invented versus the colours that already existed, the colour of the Thames and the grass in the park, and the colours of the tips of stairwells early in the morning. Maybe you can try not to think where you've seen this idea before, which artist/writer 'did that two years ago'; maybe you can try not to say 'that's like a cross between (fashionable author) and (fashionable author).

Maybe we'll even forget we can read, forget we ever watched TV, looked at a painting or heard a pop record, just for a moment. Because, after that moment passes, can you imagine the feeling of remembering?

Francis Morgan

Photographs: Scot Wishart

A brief history of…

Our retro fashion expert sings the praises of big knickers…

19th Century: Drawers

In Jane Austen's time, ladies rarely wore panties. Think of all those Empire Line frocks with nothing underneath – *ooh la la*! If knickers were worn they were, by today's standards, rather risqué. Drawers consisted of two tubes of fabric (cotton, fine lawn, crepe de chine or silk) cut wide and full and gathered onto a waistband. They tied at the front and were always – steady, boys – open at the crotch.

Drawers were not commonly worn until the 1840s, when the crinoline came in. This hooped steel contraption had a habit of rising up above the wearer's head when she sat down, leading to a sharp rise in the popularity of drawers, and the speedy invention of the gusset.

Early 20th Century: Knickerbockers

Drawers were precious things, and were passed from mother to daughter – stigma attached to 2nd hand pants then! Longer drawers gathered at the knee were also popular. After World War 1, these knickerbockers gradually became shorter to match the new skirt lengths.

1920s: Camiknickers and French Style Knickers

The 20s saw the invention of rayon (viscose), a fabric made from cellulose of pine and hemlock trees. Rayon resembled silk, but was cheaper. A new style of undies was born – camiknickers. This combination of camisole and drawers (basically a princess petticoat with a gusset or flap between the legs) was loose and shapeless, de-emphasising the figure in accordance with the fashions of the time, which themselves reflected women's increased emancipation. Wide French style knickers were also popular.

1930s: Pants/Panties

Knicker-lets became shorter as the thirties wore on. This new shape was known as pants or panties. In 1939 a patent was grated to the British Nylon Spinners, who mixed petroleum, natural gas, air and water to produce the first synthetic fabric, nylon. Nylon was durable, cheap, and popular. Underwear's heirloom days were numbered.

1940s: Woolly and Lacy Pants

In the 40s and 50s knickers continued to be designed in the French style, made of plain and printed nylon and acetate trimmed with nylon frills or lace. Strict rationing (1 pair of pants was 3 coupons) meant that girls who wanted new saucy lingerie for their gentleman friends had to get handy with the knitting needles. In 1949 Miss "Gorgeous Gussie" Moran introduced sex to the centre court at Wimbledon, by wearing a pair of frilly lace panties designed by Teddy Tinling throughout the

knickers

ladies' tournament. This instigated a tradition of unabashed lechery among male sports journalists towards female tennis players which continues to this day. History does not record whether Gorgeous Gussie purchased her pants at Fredericks of Hollywood, the legendary lingerie store opened by Frederick N Mellinger in 1946, but had she ventured there, she could have acquired a matching open point cup bra in Passion Red, Midnight Black or Lilac to wear with a beauty Plunge Bedtime Baby Doll in Hot Pink, and really driven the sports hacks wild.

1950s: The Pantie Girdle

The rationing of WW2 and the shortage of cotton and silk was followed by the mass manufacture of artificial fibres. Nylon

manufacturers DuPont invented Lycra (light than rubber, yet stronger) in 1959. It was incorporated into the tight fitting pantie girdles of the fifties which, along with distinctive cone shaped bra cups with whirlpool stitching, reintroduced a more womanly silhouette, reflecting women's return to the home after the excitement of war work.

1960s: Bikini Pants

As skirts got shorter, pants got smaller. Generally made of stretch nylon yarn, 60s pants featured strong patterns in hues of lime, purple and orange, usually simultaneously. Disposable paper pants were launched in 1969, but their popularity was short-lived, and the fad had died by the mid-70s.

1970s/80s: Briefs

As fashions became tighter and more clinging, pants became briefs – and they were. Briefs were gathered at the hip rather than at the waist, and were made in stretch lace, knitted simples and cotton polyester. The 80s was the decade that saw the G-string move from the stripper's podium to the high street, where they have been dividing opinion – and buttocks – ever since.

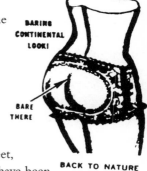

BARING CONTINENTAL LOOK!

BARE THERE

BACK TO NATURE

1990s: Tummy Trimmers

Pants can new perform the function of the 50s pantie girdle, flattening stomachs, smoothing hips and whittling waists. Triumph have even made a kind of Wonderbra for arses – lifting and separating the buttocks for a youthful line.

Anne-Marie Payne

A Flea in Sodom

Like Le Corbusier, André Breton's relationship to Paris was iconoclastic. But whereas Le Corbusier sought to raze the city and replace it with his modernist vision of utopia, Breton sought to make 'irrational embellishments' in which dreams would intervene in practical affairs. For instance, the Arc de Triomphe was to be blown up, after being buried in a mountain of manure. The Vendôme column was to be replaced by a factory chimney being climbed by a naked woman, and the Opéra transformed into a fountain spouting perfume. The towers of Nôtre-Dame were to be swapped with

Saint-Ouen flea market, 1928

an enormous glass *cruet*, one of the bottles filled with blood, the other with sperm. The cathedral itself was to become a sexual school for virgins. The flea market, however, was to remain unchanged, perhaps because it was irrational already.

On the one hand, in the Surrealist *objét trouvé*, the ready-made, kitsch-ridden city breaches the sanctity of high art and culture; on the other, in the flea market, the Surrealists found the whiff of exception to a thoroughly planned urban environment, the mainstay of a commercial culture in which everyone particpates and nobody is exempt. On Sundays, Breton would visit flea markets in search of provocative clutter; in Nadja he writes of Saint-Ouen, a flea market in Paris: 'I go there often, searching for objects that can be found nowhere else: old-fashioned, broken, useless, almost incomprehensible, even perverse'. For the Surrealists, a shiny, self-confident commodity culture is both revealed and ridiculed by the older, less self-conscious and more precarious commerce found at the flea market. Here, a crowd of petty traders sell old commodities of every description,

broken, mismatched and chaotically combined; commodities past luxuriating in shop windows, past seeming to stretch and swell under the glow of advertising. The flea market amounts to a cheapening of bourgeois culture.

Today, Parisian flea markets remain colourful, evocative places of ceaseless movement and incident, though the largest ones, like the Saint-Ouen markets at the limit of the 18th Arrondissement, are also the most established and integrated. Here licensed stallholders fix price tags to goods neatly organized into types or even displayed. Far more interesting are the flea markets at Porte de Montreuil, where old clothing is sold – by weight, and (for bric-a-brac) at Porte des Vanves, a smaller yet heavily policed market, the consequence of opposition from local residents. The *marché aux puces* are distinct in both temporal and geographical terms. Temporally, while Sunday trading restrictions have been relaxed, the Sabbath has long since been the flea market's main trading day. Spatially, the markets attach themselves to the periphery, at the old gateways to Paris, once the domicile of the chiffonniers, the city's rag pickers.

Courtyard of a rag-and-bone man, Paris 1910

The rag picker was a stallholder at some of the earliest flea markets: the Puces de Saint-Ouen, for instance, have as their origin a market formed in 1841, where rag pickers hawked furniture, apparel and other debris gleaned from the dustbins of the rich. In popular mythology, rag picking was linked to crime and the spread of disease, and municipal measures were frequently taken to curb the practice, reflecting today's constant striving to control *colpartage* wherever it appears, whether in flea markets, car boot sales or on the pavement. Eugène Atget showed a persistent, though fast disappearing underclass when he photographed rag-and-bone men and their families in the suburbs of Paris before the First World War.

While the Surrealists found a power for radicalism in the flea market, Marxist critics like Walter Benjamin looked for radicalism in one of its oldest inhabitants, finding a metaphor for subversiveness in the rag picker. He argued that all radicals could see something of themselves in a *métier* which by exploiting the very limits of bourgeois culture defined itself: 'the chiffonnier is the most provocative figure of human poverty. Lumpenproletarian in a double sense, both dressed in rags and occupied with them'. If the rag picker's rummaging through the city's refuse speaks to a wider culture of opposition, this is precisely because the figure presents itself as beyond the pale, for only in the most marginal of forms may a diverse body recognize itself.

At the same time, there are problems with looking for critical or subversive potential in marginalia, for capitalism seeks to relocate its margins at its centre. Irving Wohlfarth has argued that today 'rag-collecting is no longer a metaphor for destructive, revolutionary activity', being 'either (as in the case of third-world countries, bag-ladies and clochards) a matter of sheer survival, or else (in affluent Western societies) synonymous with *la mode rétro*, the fashion for flea-markets, the nostalgia for quilts, the restoration of clutter'. If spontaneity flees from a Disney-like, image-driven environment, the question is whether the same can be said of its blindspots and marginalia. The fate of Surrealism reminds us of how the flea market *trouvaille* can become the fashion boutique accessory.

**Ayman Solene
and Chris Turner**

Rag-and-bone, Paris, 1913

White jeans

Orange rugby shirt

Old Ted Baker shirt

Rainbow-coloured waistcoat

Shop

Shop Dropping means exactly the opposite to shop lifting. The term was invented by Polly Wiseman, and her idea was to leave clothes in clothes shops. *Cheap Date* decided to give a little bit more to the world in the form of specially selected items from a £1 bin-liner of clothes. As they say nothing is really for free, we thought we'd get some advertising in the process, writing, in puff paint, large *Cheap Date* logos on each of the clothes-to-be-dropped. Then Polly, Tallboy the photographer and I hit the high street stores of Covent Garden, reasonably nervous and not sure whether it was illegal. We even tried to dress smart to mingle invisibly, and just to make sure the clothes looked truly incongrous, we trod on them first.

Olive leather & suede shorts

Playing it cool

Photographs: Tallboy

Dropping

For goody-goody me, doing it was exhilarting, but it was easy! No-one noticed, even when we put them overtly in their window display. What happened to the clothes? We didn't stick around long enough to see. They probably just created a bit of confusion when spotted. But who knows? Maybe they were shop lifted.

The process: in Next

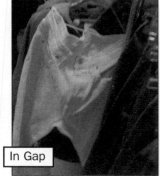

In Gap

In Diesel

Ted Baker shirt returned to it's home

Duffer of St George's new window display

NICOLE FARHI

Hidden from staff behind screen, but cheering up passers-by

PATTI PALLADIN

How come Chrissie Hynde's famous and you're not?

Hey, I'm infamous and she's not! (HA HA) Hell, fame and success is just another of life's intricate equations. More often than not, timing and luck play the most relevance. I suppose, if you want to parallel me to Chris, I'd have to say that while she was playing, I was busy living it. One is industry friendly and one just isn't! My lifestyle was perhaps too wild/too real for public consumption, but frankly my experiences have my provided me with a wealth of knowledge about myself and about life. I certainly have a handle on where my bottom line is, and that's a commodity that money cannot buy. I suppose too that fundamentally I am quite a private person and was therefore prepared to avoid going through "puberty" in public at all costs. I think also I sub-consciously fought against the pomposity and court-jesterism of fame and success which is rife in young stardom. It's just so fucking lame – Young stars are given a huge podium from which to speak and more often than not they have FUCK ALL to say. On that level it is clearly a waste of time and money and it is tedious. I suppose too, my unwillingness to compromise didn't help. I have always felt that I'll do what the fuck I like and if by chance the rest of the known world digs it, well, Great! But, I have since come to my senses on the "chance" factor – it's more like, 'Yeah, if someone whacks a huge wedge into pushing it…' – and then of course timing is so very important, Like I say in my track *Running with the Pack* "If ya run run runnin' out in front – or way down at the back – don't mean nothin' anyhow, ya still ain't runnin' the the pack" – Who knows, it may all click into sync and presto! Superstardom!! – (HA HA) Kidding aside, Let's face it, at the end of the day it's not about fame/success/status. It's who you really are that counts. If you are famous and an ego crazed narcissistic scumbag, well, then you're just a fucking famous ego crazed narcissistic scumbag!! A billion faceless people may adore you but they don't really know you – it's a controlled and safe situation. If all you have is this global blanket of worshippers and a staff of hand picked "yes men" – you're in fuckin' trouble. Surely the more successful one becomes, the more essential it is to maintain a sound personal life to keep you in check. So

Patti with Hagstrom

Photograph: Kate Simon

often this is foolishly overlooked and the resulting delusions eventually morph into depression, paranoia etc – you're in the red zone and then the Priory for a month.

Do you think there might be a *young* elite today, doing all the cool stuff, or is your generation the last?

Cool stuff will always come thru. If you don't believe that ya may as will start chewin' thru ya wrists now! Yeah, the rate of percentage does vary, in

retrospect it is clear that some generations are "cooler" than others n' yeah, I'm sure as hell glad about the slice o' time I was dealt! Man, there will always be characters who are inherantly "cool" n' frankly age is irrelevant – take Bill Boroughs, Mac Rebennac, Dylan – on the other hand the inherantly LAME are out there in droves n' man those fuckers could live a thousand lifetimes – won't matter – they'll still be fuckin' LAME. This list is a lot longer n' I won't bore you! (HA HA).

To Londoners, New York seems incredible. Why did you move to London?

Yeah, New York is pretty incredible and although I wouldn't want to live there, it's always good for a quick-hit vignette! I do feel really lucky to have been born in NYC and to have 'learned the ropes' there. I grew up in Brooklyn, just a step over the Williamsberg Bridge. It was the tail end of the style-conscious gangs with names like the Hellburners and the Phantom Lords or The ElleryBops. Jerry Nolan was from my neighbourhood, he was a Young Lord. The knowledge gathered during those

formative years was enough to get you through any scenario. It was pure Scorcese. The Village was just a shot away and the lunacy was starting to kick in a big way. An extraordinary collection of crazies stumbled between the Fillmore, Max's, the Cafe Wha, Nobody's, The Crazy House etc – Hendrix was the resident party fucker at the Cafe Wha – There were "smoke ins" in Thompson Squre Park with freaks like Moondog and The Fugs providing the music. Everyone was drinkin' the stuff called Romilar, cutting school n' hangin' out. Max's was superb at that time. You'd gaze across the room and see the likes o' Mo Tucker, Lee Radizwell, a Baglady, Holly Woodlawn, Truman Capote, a banker, a homeless wino poet, Tuli Kappenberg, David Johansen and Tiny Tim sittin' 'round the same table sparring over a bowl of chickpeas! It was truly Fellini-esque – a congregation of individuals all sporting their own distinct concept of themselves. Unlike today, it don't matter where you are or what the joint is, you walk in and there's a mob of MTV identicats.

The British thing was in full swing and I was wearing a lot of of Jeanny's and Countdown stuff, velvet suits, chiffon shirts, hats with plummage n' snakeskin boots and actually had trannys make me a pair of boots that were covered in little appliqued leather numerals – my phone number. Man, were we all total clothes gluttons and I quickly sussed that it made big time sense to go cop my threads in London cause the NY branches were selling the stuff for like 5 x the price. By now I'd had quie a few UK friends and open invites. It was ideal – a cheap flight to a 10 day shoppng frenzy, the Speakeasy, mandrax and then home. Then one day I left my MGBGT and my afghan hound with my mom's dad, headed for London to fuckup a new pair o' boots and never went back.

When did you realise you wanted to play rock'n'roll?

I suppose the 'Murray K' shows planted dthe seed, seeing the Shangri-Las, Ronnettes, Otis, Wilson Picket etc – But the British thing was the icing on the cake – and of couse Hendrix. Yeah those boys have

got a lot to answer for, there'd probably be twice as many scientists, doctors n' lawyers etc on the planet if them bad boys never showed up!

Do you look back fondly on Snatch?

Yes, absolutely, it was great fun collaborating with Judy, she's quite an amazing being – extremely bright, extremely creative and superbly strange. Between us we devised some pretty out-there ideas. The Snatch stuff was really about ideas, unfortunately we never really had sufficient funding to realize and polish it. We met on a trans-Atlantic phone call. She was here in London! hanging out at a mutual friend's photographic studio when I rang to say I was pulling into London that week. So my mate goes "Hey, I'm here with this babe Judy, you guys

With friend Anita Pallenberg ,taken for her cover version of 'Memo From Turner'

will really hit it off" and puts her on the line. After a quick yap she asks if I know about the Norma Kamali high wasted trousers and could I score her a pair. Of course I was hip to the great early Kamali stuff and said "What Size?" We both instantly passed the test!! We had a "fire n' ice" relationship and juggled the good cop / bad cop routine when doing business. Obviously I'm very proud of things like 'RAF', our collaboration with Eno and the legendary All I Want Is Lurve. Who knows, if we run into each other and the conditions are right there's always the threat of an additional Snatch offering.

I don't really know for sure, but you seem to have avoided becoming a bad drug addict. How did you manage this?

Oooops Kira, research loophole! You must be fuckin' kidding me darlin' – 'ere – refer back to question one, it proves my point about early fame n' going through "puberty" in public – lets just say, yeah "I sang in that church" or "there was a time when I was a very Expensive Date!" or, how 'bout "Been around the block n' got to know the neighbourhood reeeeal well" – next question please.

The Copycats album was not only before it's time, but great. Are you pleased with it?

Absolutely, I'm really proud of that record – it's pure unadulterated honest fun. It's not marred by some poxy social political statement, its' not a self importance ego thing, it's not art, it doesn't proport to be anything other than a selection of tunes from a given period. At the time Johnny wanted us to form a band together, he was in so-so shape and staying with me. In theory, yeah it was s cool idea but I was just too hip to Johnny and knew it would be a fucking nightmare, with me doing most of the work. As much as I really wanted to, I too was a little unstable and couldn't see past the hassle of auditioning players, rehearsing and arranging the new material etc and said "No way". There's still some unrecorded material that we wrote during that time which I'm now eager to nail – but anyway John was hellbent for us to do something together and was lusting for the advance. He suggested the covers thing which I wasn't at all keen on, but he hassled me enough so I agreed but only if I produced it and had it written into my contract that I could bunk at any time if it all got too stupid. What's interesting about Copycats is the enormous spectrum of material. It really is rather a deranged cross section – from the Seeds to Burt Bacharach to Screamin' Jay to the Shangri las, Dion and Jules Stern etc. I dreaded the possibility of creating some naff Pub Rock show-band covers thing. As producer, I fought like a demon for the time and budget to enable me to give each tune the attention to detail it

required and deserved. Johnny loved Copycats, he was really really proud of it which needless to say makes me very happy indeed. It was his lasst studio album.

Will we ever see another Johnny Thunders or Jerry Nolan? Do you think people that cool can still exist or would they just be marketed into wankers?

In one word – NO! – and as far as marketing goes – NO! again. Quite simply "not marketable." Too much too soon! Even all the stuff that has appeared since their deaths is just sycophantic watered down jive. The NY Dolls book which has just appeared is well, frankly, LAME. I was really annoyed at seeing quotes from Johnny and Jerry in it – Man, those guys have been dead for nearly 10 years, where the

Patti with
Johnny Thunders
Photograph: Lee
Black Childers

fuck do you come up with quotes that are shoved in context with all the other shit as though they are actually party to contributing to the book. It's journalistic trickery. They most be spinning in their graves! and now, there's talk of "The Johnny Thunders Story" movie – NURSE!! now ya'all know that's gonna be a real load o' shit! I avoid this stuff like the fucking plague. Lets face it, these "authors"/ "filmakers" etc can't possibly really get it – like I say in my track *Showdown* "They never lived this way, they'll never die this way" so what the fucking do they know?!! Johnny used to have a great name for these people: "SPONGES!"

Do you ever find it hard to feel motivated?

Sure, so often the mundane bullshit of day to day life depleats you - not to mention the nonsense business buraucracy. Bull. All this only stuns you for a moment every now and then. The only thing that really threw me was my mother's death recently. She was ust so incredible – the best – but she love music, played a bit of mandolin and was always supportive and proud of whatever I did. It's coming up to 2 years now and I'm finally up n' dustin' myself off from the blow. I now feel very motivated, by her spirit and really want to do it! Yeah, I'm ready to rock.

For all Patti's answers including the story of her infamous 'Stones' project, write to us!

The Groom

The Bride

Everyone was happily hanging out...

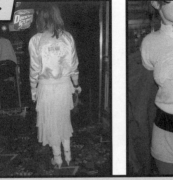

... until bad news arrived in the form of Putney's brother Kenneth

I don't think Papa's going to like this...

It's done!

Suddenly, all the girls sensed the hitherto unseen yet exceptional sexual magnetism emanating from Kenneth...

Here's some money!

...and pounced!

WOW!!!!!!

You are now one of us!

You are God!

I must have you!

126

She's probably lying on the pavement!

A contetti of silver stars was showered upon Putney and Jett

Their cosmic happiness only a start fo fulfilling all their dreams.

Forever

The End

Starring:
Eric Goulden as Graeme Turner
Annabel Mullion as Gloria Turner
John Lycett-Green as Kenneth Turner
John Spencer as Jett Blak
Bernie Zimmerframe as the priest
Rob and Gavin of the Cheetahs as Jett's mates.
And introducing *Daisy de Villeneuve* as Putney Turner
Wedding guests: Lucy Woods, Doune, Katie, Iris, Max, Matthew ...
Screenplay: Kira Jolliffe
Director: **Poppy de Villeneuve**

Slab-O-Concrete Publications

"Underground publisher featuring some of the best and freakiest alternative books in comic strip and print format" –The Big Issue

Sugar Buzz
'Live At Budokan'
Woodrow Phoenix & Ian Carney
ISBN 1 899866 33 7 • £6.50/$12.50
400% of your recommended daily allowance of partially hydrogenated humour, hi-jinks and general lunacy with Urbane Gorilla, Sugar Kat, Lumbo & Lumbo, Pants Ant and many more.

Bulletins From Serbia
Aleksandar Zograf
ISBN 1 899866 31 0 • £6.50/$12.00
The email diary of a cartoonist living in Serbia during the NATO bombings in spring 1999. Dry observation mixed with personal insight into a catastrophe. An important human document. With an introduction by Terry Jones.

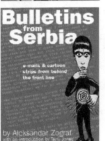

Teaching Through Trauma
Leanne franson
ISBN 1 899866 27 2 • £5.00/$9.95
Follow bi-dyke Liliane through her tragicomic life as she bounces from relationship trauma to relationship trauma. Covers first dates, sexuality, family, love, work, art, wigs and more. Who needs self-help books when you've Liliane

The GirlFrenzy Millennial
Edited by Erica Smith
ISBN 1 899866 18 3 • £6.50/$12.00
A girl's annual gone BAD! Pages filled with a glorious medley of comics, photostories, articles, interviews and more. Contributors include Megan Kelso, Roberta Gregory, Lorna Miller, Trina Robbins, Jane Graham, and more.

Lux & Alby
Martin Millar and Simon Fraser
ISBN 1 899866 24 8 • £6.95/$12.50
When Lux the Poet and Alby Starvation, famed inhabitants of Brixton, find themselves thrown together, the fabric of the universe strats to crumble. An epic comic (288 pages) from the UK's funniest writer and *2000AD*'s best artist.

Excreta
Ole Comoll Christensen
ISBN 1 899866 28 0 • £5.50/$9.95
A detective starts an investigation when he finds earwax smeared on the barrel of a gun, a vampire discovers a taste for human milk, a girl finds her luck lies in vomit, a military dictatorship is topple by pustules... it gets worse!

For more information about *Cheap Date New York* call 0966 498078 (in the UK) or visit the website at www.cheapdate.net. Other bits and pieces are available, including the complete Patti Paladin interview and Melody Foxx's entire Mills & Boon-esque story – it's romantic!

This is just a selection of our many books, send for a catalogue to find out more • Mail order: UK – post is included, send cheques to Slab-O-Concrete, PO Box 148, Hove, BN3 3DQ, UK • Overseas, please send well-concealed cash or add £5 for bank charges to clear a check in your own currency • Alternatively, all our titles can be ordered from bookstores by their ISBN numbers.